The Ultimate Girl

To Understanding and Caring for Your Body

By Isabel & Emily Lluch
• age 16 •   • age 13 •

AND THEIR PANEL OF EXPERTS

WS Publishing Group
San Diego, California

The Ultimate Girls' Guide
To Understanding and Caring for Your Body

❖

BY ISABEL & EMILY LLUCH

Published by WS Publishing Group
San Diego, California 92119
Copyright © 2009 by WS Publishing Group

Nutritional and fitness guidelines based on information provided by the United States Food and Drug Administration, Food and Nutrition Information Center, National Agricultural Library, Agricultural Research Service, and the U.S. Department of Agriculture.

Designed by: David Defenbaugh & Sarah Jang, WS Publishing Group

For inquiries:
Log on to www.WSPublishingGroup.com
E-mail info@WSPublishingGroup.com

ISBN-13: 978-1-934386-43-9

Printed in China

Table of Contents

✿ Table of Contents...............

About the Authors

Written by girls for girls!

Hey there, we're Isabel, age 16, and Emily, age 13. Even though we're sisters, we have really different styles, opinions, and interests. Yet, we both share a passion for life that makes us great girls to turn to when you have questions about your changing body and emotions. We know not every girl is totally comfortable talking to her parents or other adults about things like puberty and hygiene. And honestly, sometimes, adults just don't get it. That's why we—along with our friends and a panel of 6 experts in medicine, nutrition and fitness, dermatology, dentistry, psychology, and beauty—are here to help. We're confident that this book will answer all your big questions. And don't worry—no question is weird, funny, or embarrassing. We're dealing with the exact same issues you are!

About the Authors

All About Isabel

I'm Isabel, and I'm 16. I like girly stuff like clothes, makeup, and hair, but don't call me superficial—I'm witty, artsy, and a great friend. On the weekend, you can probably find me at a vintage clothing store, sewing, or getting a manicure with my girlfriends. Being 16, I'm still going through the physical and emotional changes that come along with puberty. But I have no problem about asking my mom or other experts to explain serious matters, like periods, breasts, or eating disorders. I know this is an awkward time in every girl's life—that's why my sister Emily and I decided to write this book.

All About Emily

Hi, I'm Emily! I'm 13 and the sporty sister. I'm a straight-A student, and I love doing anything outdoorsy, especially playing soccer. I have the greatest group of friends, both at school and on my team. My friends and coaches think I'm fearless, which makes me a good person to help answer your questions about body changes—even sort of scary topics like body odor and mood swings. Trust me, I know exactly how you feel, because I just had a talk with my mom about getting my period. I think she was more embarrassed than I was! LOL!

Together, my sister and I make an awesome team, speaking to all girls who are too scared or shy to ask about the changes puberty brings. Everything you need to know about beauty, fashion, hygiene, periods, breasts, healthy eating, staying in shape, emotions, and dealing with stress is right here in this book.

Approved by and filled with valuable information from:

Dr. Stuart Cohen, Physician

Dr. Stuart Cohen holds a medical degree from the University of Manitoba, as well as a Masters in Public Health Maternal and Child Health from San Diego State University. He has been named one of "America's Top Physicians" by the Consumer Research Council of America. Dr. Cohen practices at California's Children's Primary Care Medical Group, Inc. (www.cpcmg.medem.com).

Catherine Butler, Therapist

Catherine Butler is a Marriage and Family Therapist in La Mesa, California. A veteran of the Canadian Navy and a former middle and high school teacher, she devotes her practice to families, children and specializes in military issues. She also raises dogs for Guide Dogs of the Desert and is a Disaster Mental Health volunteer for the American Red Cross.

Dr. Richard Fitzpatrick, Dermatologist

Dr. Richard Fitzpatrick is an innovative leader in dermatology, previously named *Allure* Magazine's "Physician Who Has Most Influenced Beauty" and Sturge-Weber Society's "Physician of the Year." A Princeton University graduate, Dr. Fitzpatrick attended Emory University Medical School. He currently practices with the La Jolla Cosmetic Surgery Centre. To learn more, visit http://ljcsc.com/.

Lisa Kudra, Certified Fitness Trainer & Nutritionist

Lisa Kudra holds Clinical Nutritionist Certification from The Natural Healing Institute of Naturopathy and Personal Fitness Training Certification from the Aerobics and Fitness Association of America. She owns Get Fit with Lisa K! (www.getfitwithlisak.com), where she specializes in weight loss, athletic performance, core strengthening, holistic healthcare, and overall lifestyle improvements.

Dr. Gary Hirsh, Orthodontist

Dr. Gary Hirsh has been practicing Orthodontics and DentoFacial Orthopedics in California since 1971. He holds degrees from Georgetown University Dental School and Temple University School of Dentistry. In addition, he was a captain in the US Air Force Dental Corps, stationed at Castle Air Force Base in Merced, California.

Wendy McGill, Beautician & Fashion Expert

Style and beauty expert Wendy McGill has always had an eye for fashion and the latest hairstyles. With more than 9 years of experience in the beauty industry, she loves the ability to be creative and change the way people look and feel about themselves. McGill and her husband Jeremy currently own JDM Salon in San Diego, California (www.jdmsalon.com).

❀ About the Authors.............................

Why Every Girl Needs This Book!

If there's one thing that's true about girls, it's that we love talking with our friends. That's why we're so excited for you to meet us and our girlfriends in *The Ultimate Girls' Guide to Understanding and Caring for Your Body*.

We think this book is a unique way for teen and preteen girls like you to learn from other girls who have gone through or are going through all the same feelings, fears, and hopes. Not every girl is perfectly proportioned or athletic or popular or outgoing, but every girl our age goes through puberty and experiences pretty much the same changes and frustrations.

The Ultimate Girls' Guide to Understanding and Caring for Your Body is for girls who are on the verge of starting puberty or girls who are in the middle of it. You can even pass this book along to your parents to help them understand exactly what you're going through. Use this book to break the ice with your mom or dad—they may have some good advice for you, too! (Even though they're probably way too old to remember puberty. Ha ha!)

Throughout this book, you will get even more advice from our panel of 6 experts, who have helped us answer the most important questions girls our age have. While we're able to give you a girl's take on these issues, these experts will offer a pro's perspective as well.

To give you the best advice possible, we've done a ton of our own research. We also consulted with our parents, relatives, doctors, therapists, teachers, coaches, nutritionists, health and beauty professionals. Our answers are easy to understand and fun to read. You'll also find helpful hints, fun facts, and practical tips on every page. We want every girl to think of us as trusted friends. No girl should go through this time in her life alone!

Isn't it cool that there's finally a fun book, written by real girls, that answers all your questions (instead of those lame books they give you in sex-ed class)? We guarantee that once you read everything in *The Ultimate Girls' Guide*, you'll see that everything you're going through is normal, so you don't have to be freaked out anymore. We can't wait for you to feel so much more confident, pretty, and happy! ★

Looking Your Best

Fun, flirty, and fabulous!

Being a girl can be really hard! Don't get us wrong, we would never trade it, but girls have a lot of stuff to think about, including our weight, what to wear, and our overall appearance. These pressures come up really quickly, too! It's so weird to think how we were just little girls not long ago, and then, suddenly, we find ourselves out bra shopping!

✿ Looking Your Best ....

★ Isabel's Perspective

Physical changes are confusing and nerve-wracking. On top of that, you have to worry about being stylish and trendy, which quickly becomes a priority. Every girl deals with this stuff differently.

Learning how to dress for my body type has been very important. I mean, no one wants to see a too-tight outfit or some girl's underwear sticking out. So, learning to trade popular trends for what looks good on your body is the first lesson in fashion.

The next lesson is to hold off the pressure to wear tons of makeup for as long as possible. I'm talking about heavy eye shadow, eyeliner, and dark lipstick. These make girls our age look like they're trying too hard. To be honest, I'm one of those girls who always puts on too much makeup. Our beauty expert Wendy McGill has really helped me tone it down! She suggests wearing subtle, light colors for the "barely there" look. She said you want just enough to highlight your natural beauty. You want to look young and fresh, because that's what we are!

★ Emily's Perspective

Hey sis! I agree that you totally wear too much makeup. LOL! I'm not as much a makeup girl—to me, being pretty is more about having great hair. Not all of us are born with it, but thankfully, there are hair products that can totally fix poofy, flat, frizzy, crazy-curly, or limp hair. A great hair product goes a long way!

I also want to talk about all the pressure girls encounter when it comes to fashion. In my opinion, instead of trying to keep up with the hardcore fashionistas in your school, you should experiment with different styles until you find one that fits you. Copying other girls is the lazy way to find your style, so be cutting-edge by finding ways to dress that express your tastes and personality.

Body Types

"A girl should be two things: classy and fabulous."
~ Coco Chanel

✿ Helpful Hint

Tired of being the shortest girl in your class? Rise above it by wearing shoes with a low heel. Even the slightest lift will boost your confidence. Making this subtle change is an easy fix until you hit your growth spurt, which may happen any day now. In fact, you may even grow up to 4 inches in 1 year! So, hang in there—your time to be taller is just around the corner. In the meantime, cheat with heels!

★ The Scoop

It's totally OK if you don't look exactly like other girls. I mean, we all come in different shapes and sizes. And though it may not always be easy to choose what to wear, understanding your individual body type will give you fashion direction.

Since you're not a kid anymore, it's time to start choosing clothes for your body type, instead of just throwing on whatever's on the floor. Pear-shaped girls are bigger on the bottom. Apple-shapes are broader on the top. Girls with the same size bust and hips are hourglass-shaped. And finally, some girls are a rectangle shape, meaning they are pretty much straight up and down.

According to our fashion expert Wendy McGill, the most important component of any fashion sense is your attitude. She says, no matter what your size or shape, you should always carry yourself with confidence. If you look confident, you'll always look good.

❧ Body Types ....

⚙ Helpful Hint

Don't compare yourself to other girls! It will only make you feel bad. Instead, remember that everyone goes through body changes. So, you may never look like the girl sitting next to you, and that's OK! Truthfully, that girl you admire probably wishes she looked like someone else—maybe you!

🌀 Fun Fact

We worry we are getting fat, however, most of us are just going through the normal filling-out process that happens during puberty. So, unless your current weight is 10 percent or more than what is recommended for your age and height, don't sweat it! Eat healthy and exercise and your body will even out eventually.

★ May Ling's Question: Fit or Fat?

Lately I notice that my clothes are tight around the middle—especially my pants. It also seems like my shirt keeps riding up. I hate it, because it makes me feel like I'm getting fat! I still weigh the same, so I don't get it. How can I weigh the same but not fit into my normal clothes anymore?

Emily Says

I totally know how you feel, May Ling! I play soccer and when I grew out of my uniform, I freaked out thinking I was getting fat.

When I asked my coach about it she said that I was developing hips. She said my weight was shifting around. This is why even though I went up a whole pants size, I still weighed the same. Like my coach said, this means your body is just doing what it's supposed to do.

Even though it stinks buying bigger clothes, it is the best option—don't try to stuff your new hips into old jeans. You'll look like an ice cream cone! Once you get over the sticker shock of larger sizes, you'll look great.

Isabel Says

Hey May Ling! Emily's totally right; your body is just filling out into its natural shape. Why don't you just look at this as an excuse to get all new clothes! ☺

★ Katie's Question: Too Tall!

I have always been the tallest girl in my class. But now I tower over everyone, even the boys! Is it normal to be this tall? How can I make myself blend in more? I hate that I stand out so much.

Isabel Says

I feel you Katie—I was one of the tallest kids in my class for a long time. It's hard to be so tall, especially when you're bigger than most of the guys. But start thinking about being tall as a beautiful thing. I mean, it is the number one requirement in the modeling industry!

Emily Says

OK Katie, until your modeling career gets going, make small changes to accommodate your height. Don't slouch, because that lets everyone know you're uncomfortable—plus it's bad for your spine. You can wear flats, like tennis shoes or sandals to downplay your height, but I say, rock the heels anyway. If boys make jokes about your height, it's only because they wish they were taller!

Isabel Says

Don't worry girlie—you won't always tower above everyone else. Your growth spurt just came before the others! The other kids caught up to me in about a year. Soon you'll be the one wearing heels to look taller!

✿ Helpful Hint

Curvy girls will look cute in dark pants that have a flare or bootcut leg. Jeans with tight ankles make girls with bigger butts look like inverted triangles, which is not a good look! Or, try a wrap-dress—they really flatter curvy bodies and are easy to accessorize. Also, wear shirts that reach your hips to give the illusion of a longer torso. Curves are feminine and pretty!

◉ Did You Know?

Whenever you feel bad about your body, concentrate on what you're good at, like running, drawing, or sewing. Remembering that you're really good at something that doesn't have to do with looks makes you feel awesome, instead of insecure.

❀ Body Types ....

☞ Expert's Point of View

Tips and Advice from Dr. Stuart Cohen

Though your body is going to change quite a bit over the next several years, your body type will always remain the same.

For example, if you are "big-boned," you will always weigh a little bit more than other girls your size. But this does not mean you are fat! Don't obsess over your weight, because the numbers on the scale can fluctuate from day to day depending on what time of day it is or how much water you've had to drink. Instead, focus on how your body looks proportionally. If your weight is distributed evenly, then you will look great, no matter what the scale says.

Accept that there is nothing you can do to change your body type, and then embrace it. Indeed, though your frame is determined by genetics, your attitude and level of physical fitness are most definitely up to you. These make all the difference in the way you look.

Wrapping It Up

Finding the perfect swimsuit can be so hard! Stick with what flatters your body: Try boyshorts or a skirted suit if you're shy about your thighs. Tankinis are cute and cover the stomach. Ruffles can play up a small chest, while a halter top gives good support for bigger boobs. And girls of every size look pretty in bikinis—just make sure it's OK with your parents! ★

Hair

"Forget not that the earth delights to feel your bare feet and the winds long to play with your hair."
~ Kahlil Gibran

⚓ Helpful Hint

Gel, mousse, and hairspray leave product build-up on your hair. To remove this accumulated muck, wash your hair with a clarifying shampoo and massage it into your scalp for a full 30 seconds. Also, many hair products contain alcohol, which can dry out your scalp. For a super-itchy scalp, use a special scalp conditioner with peppermint or tea tree oil. Let it sit for 5 minutes before rinsing.

★ The Scoop

It may seem like you have enough to think about before school let alone adding hair care to your list of morning rituals. But having good hair-hygiene habits is important! For most of us, this means washing and conditioning our hair 4 or 5 times a week and using appropriate products to style it daily.

Choosing hair care products can be overwhelming, but you can narrow down your options based on your hair type—long, medium, short, curly, wavy, or straight. Girls with long hair should use a wide brush to prevent strands from breaking. Girls with short hair can use their fingers for styling. And every girl should be extra-careful combing their hair when it's wet—that's when hair is most vulnerable and can be damaged easily.

Also, allow your hair to air-dry a few times a week instead of using a blow dryer. This will minimize frizzy hair and dry, split ends.

✿ Hair ....

★ Haley's Question: Ponytails

I have really long hair. It annoys me a lot, but I'm afraid to cut it, so I pull it back in a ponytail almost every day. I'm starting to get bored with this look, plus, the ponytail sometimes makes my head sore. Is there another style that's easy and will keep my hair out of my face?

Emily Says

Well, you don't want to get stuck wearing your hair the same way every single day, Haley. And you're right, a tight ponytail can pull on your scalp. Beauty expert Wendy McGill says that wearing your hair back all the time can cause it to break near the elastic. I wear a ponytail for sports, and she told me to give my hair a rest by wearing it down a few hours each day. So I try to remember to take it down when I'm home.

Isabel Says

Hi Haley! A cute style to try is to wear a headband or wrap a colorful scarf around your hair, tying it underneath. You'll give your head a break and look pretty (plus you can also hide dirty hair on the days you don't have time to wash it!).

Emily Says

Isabel's right—hair accessories make for quick pick-me-ups. I also throw on a hat on busy days. Boys love girls in baseball caps!

❀ Helpful Hint

To deal with oily or lackluster locks, wash hair frequently with a clear shampoo that contains panthenol—an ingredient that penetrates hair to give it lift. If you need to use conditioner to get a comb through your hair, use it sparingly and only on the ends—avoid putting it on your scalp since this will make hair look greasy.

👁 Did You Know?

Hair has phases of growth; about 15 percent of your hair is resting while the other 85 percent is growing or dividing cells for new growth. In general, hair grows around 6 inches each year. While you can't speed up growth, if you're dying for long hair, get a trim every 6 to 8 weeks to keep ends neat and healthy.

★ Ashanti's Question: Frizzies

It seems like no matter what I do my super-curly hair is always frizzy by the end of the day. It drives me crazy! I only wash my hair every other day so that oils can build up and make it heavier, but it doesn't really help. I use heavy-duty conditioner as well as gel. I'm starting to feel like a poodle head! Oh, and rainy days are the worst. What can I do to keep my hair frizz-free?

Isabel Says

That's rough! Wendy McGill says, to keep crazy-curly hair under control, use leave-in conditioner every day. Even if you don't wash your hair, wet it and put on leave-in conditioner. She said it will totally make a difference.

Emily Says

Hey Ashanti, I have another idea—I've heard you can put a little bit of hand lotion on your palms and run them over the ends of your hair.

Isabel Says

I'm with you Emily! The lotion will definitely weigh down your ends so they don't poof out.

And on extra-humid days, bring an elastic band with you—a bun is always a cute option when things get crazy-frizzy.

❀ Helpful Hint

Many of the issues we have with our hair have to do with sticking with hairstyles that are wrong for our lifestyles. For example, if you play sports, you don't want bangs hanging in your face and getting all sweaty. Try cutting long layers instead. They can easily be pulled back. It might be scary to try a new style, but you just might find something easier that you love!

👁 Girl to Girl

Girls with super-dry hair have to take measures to avoid looking like Frankenstein's bride! Shampoos that have an oil-base, like olive or nut oils, work best. And definitely rinse with cool water for a clean rinse that leaves hair shiny.

✿ Hair ....

Tips and Advice from Beauty Expert Wendy McGill

Great-looking hair takes effort, but it doesn't have to cost a lot. For example, girls with uncolored hair can add a teaspoon of baking soda to their shampoo to remove product build-up (skip this if you have color in your hair, as it will cause it to fade). Do this once a week and you'll notice that your hair is bouncy and soft.

Frequent blow-drying and sun exposure will dry out your hair and make it more prone to breakage and split ends. Use a deep conditioning treatment for up to 20 minutes once a week to put valuable moisture back into damaged hair.

Also, your hair needs sun protection, just like your skin. Look for products with sunscreen or UV filters to protect your hair from breakage and sun damage.

Another easy way to keep your hair healthy and shiny is to buy a boar-bristled brush. The natural bristles aren't damaging and will make your hair really smooth and beautiful!

Wrapping It Up

One of the hardest things about hair is making it work for any occasion. For example, Emily needs to be able to pull her hair back when she does something active, but also have it look nice at events like church or a holiday dinner. Make your hair work for all occasions by having the right products. Spend at least 10 minutes on your hair. You will feel better when you put the effort in and take pride in your look. ★

Makeup

"Look your best—who said love is blind?"
~ Mae West

⭐ The Scoop

Just because other girls at your school are wearing foundation or lipstick doesn't mean you have to. Makeup is a really personal choice. If you're comfortable without it, wait until you're ready. Over time, makeup use can cause pimples and even wrinkles, so go without it for as long as you can.

The key to pretty makeup is keeping it barely noticeable. If you do want to add some color to your lips and eyes, make sure it is light and blends with your skin tone. If you try too many colors, you'll look like it's Halloween!

There is no excuse for caking makeup on. Opt for subtle enhancements. For example, just use one coat of brown mascara to give lashes length and bring out your eye color. Instead of lipstick, wear clear or nude gloss. It moisturizes your lips and makes them plump and shiny! Finally, avoid thick, heavy foundation. Instead, use liquid concealer that is the same color as your skin to hide blemishes.

⚓ Helpful Hint

If you're not ready to use a lot of makeup on your eyes but want to look a bit more glam, use an eyelash curler. This must-have tool is in every stylish girl's makeup bag. It is easy to use and adds volume and shape to flat eyelashes.

For an extra touch of allure, use one coat of mascara before curling, and one after. Your eyes will pop!

★ Kiki's Question: Cover-Up

I'm starting to break out a lot on my forehead and chin. I've tried both liquid foundation and powders, but nothing seems to cover zits without making them worse. Is there anything I can use to hide pimples without making more?

Isabel Says

I hear you! I break out and am constantly trying to find ways to hide the zits. I finally learned from dermatologist Dr. Fitzpatrick that the foundation I was using was actually clogging my pores, which caused more breakouts. Now, I only buy makeup that is "non-comedogenic," which means it won't clog your pores.

To hide zits, I really like using a concealer stick. It makes my skin look flawless and is easy to apply to just a few places.

Emily Says

Ew, zits are so frustrating! Since I don't like makeup, I just use a tinted zit cream that matches my skin tone to cover up blemishes. You just dab it on each pimple instead of putting makeup all over your face, which can make you break out more.

You might have to try a few different things before you find the best products. Keep experimenting—you'll find the right one.

✿ Helpful Hint

Every girl needs the right tools for applying makeup. Cotton swabs and sponges can be used to apply everything from concealer to eye shadow or correct mascara mistakes. Use a fresh cotton swab daily to avoid spreading bacteria, but you can reuse sponges. They're great because you can simply wash them with water and mild soap.

Girl to Girl

Don't share your compact! Letting your BFF use your powder to blot out afternoon shine is unsanitary. Worse, oil and potential bacteria from her face may cause you to break out when you use it next. Makeup is very personal and should be used only by you.

★ Katie's Question: Pale Face

I have really pale skin, so I used some blush to give my face a little color. I used pink powder blush, but when I put it on I looked like a creepy doll! The blush was way too pink and looked totally fake. How can I add color to my face without looking weird or without spending tons at a tanning salon?

Emily Says

Blush can make you look bright and healthy, but learning how to correctly use it is a bit of a science. I recommend starting with bronzers, which are easy and give a summery glow. Bronzers are great, because they give you a sun-kissed tan without the expense (or skin cancer risk, yikes!) of actual tanning. Bronzers also give an all-over color boost, whereas blush is just applied on your cheeks. The thing with bronzers, though, is to make sure you get the right shade. It should be close to your own skin tone.

Isabel Says

That's a great point Emily! Otherwise, you'll end up with an orange face, and we all want to avoid the Oompa-Loompa look (ahem, I'm thinking of a certain celebrity). When you use bronzer, tap most of the powder off the brush and use a light swirling motion when you apply it. It won't take long to get the hang of it!

✿ Helpful Hint

How you prepare your face before putting on makeup is just as important as the products you use. Wash your face with a gentle cleanser every day and remember to moisturize—this includes your lips! We all know how gross it looks when lipgloss is peeling off dry, flaky lips. Condition your kisser with lip balm before putting any colored lip stuff on.

🥔 Did You Know?

It's important to look great **and** shop with a conscience. There are lots of cosmetics companies that don't test their products on animals. Nothing is prettier than a girl who cares about the world around her. To find animal-friendly cosmetics, visit www.caringconsumer.com.

✿ Makeup  ....

> ## 👉 Expert's Point of View
>
> ### Tips and Advice from Beauty Expert Wendy McGill
>
> Makeup is a tool that should enhance your already youthful, radiant appearance. So make this your makeup motto: Less is more!
>
> Of course, it's fun to get wild and dramatic with makeup now and then, but save the heavy applications and glittery products for Halloween and slumber parties.
>
> Showing up to school in red lipstick, blue eye shadow, and pink blush will definitely make you look scary. The way you can tell if your makeup is done right is to ask yourself if it blends together and looks natural.
>
> Take your time and take chances while experimenting, but always err on the side of soft and subtle. If you want to amp it up just a bit, try light shades of powder eyeshadow or lipgloss that have a little bit of sparkle. You will get a nice glow that looks natural and pretty. Another easy tip is to rub cream blush into the apples of your cheeks—it will go on fairly sheer, more like a soft wash of color. Finally, using your fingers to apply most makeup is a surefire way to keep it subtle.

Wrapping It Up

Some girls are so good with makeup, it's like they were born with mascara in their hand. But most of us have to learn how to use the stuff. We taught ourselves by experimenting. You can buy shades of inexpensive eye shadows and lipglosses and play around with colors. But, no matter how you feel about makeup, the whole point is to be comfortable. So if you don't like how you look or feel, skip it and go *au natural*! ★

Fashion

"Fashions fade. Style is eternal."
~ Yves St. Laurent

★ The Scoop

It's hard to imagine having to think about one more thing besides our grades, friends, and boys, right? Well, add "what to wear" to your list, because fashion choices can make or break a girl's entire look. So, get schooled on how to dress, what not to wear, and what works for your body type.

In fact, dressing for your particular shape is more important than any piece of clothing you put on your body. But being fashionable doesn't mean becoming a slave to the latest trends. This can get cheesy, not to mention expensive, as the styles change. Stock your wardrobe with mostly classic pieces and just a few trendy pieces, and you will always be in style. Examples include jeans, fitted t-shirts, a white button-down shirt, fitted jacket, sandals, boots, and cute accessories. With these, your look will always be in.

Plus, when you don't know what to wear, you can just combine a few of these classic pieces to create a foolproof outfit!

❀ Helpful Hint

Shopping for clothes doesn't have to break the bank. To save some bucks, shop at thrift stores. Vintage clothes are hip, chic, and unique. Look for cool stuff like cowboy boots, dresses from the '70s, and costume jewelry. A big plus is that thrifted clothes, like jeans, come perfectly broken in. Also, consider doing a monthly clothing swap with your girlfriends. This is fun and saves everyone money!

★ Aleah's Question: Brand Names

I get that clothes matter, but the girls in my school act like the only thing that counts is "who" you're wearing. I don't wear anything with a name! My parents won't let me buy clothes that cost a lot of money. I never cared before, but I'm starting to feel like a total loser. How can I keep up with the fashionable girls in my school and still respect my parents' budget?

Isabel Says

There are some things parents do not understand Aleah, and the importance of designer labels on jeans and bags is definitely one of them.

Luckily, you can find designer labels at stores like TJ Maxx, Ross, Marshall's, Off Fifth, and Nordstrom Rack. These stores sell name-brand clothing for much less. Also, cruise clearance racks at your favorite stores, and shop a season ahead or behind (i.e., get bathing suits at the end of the season and save them for next year).

Emily Says

Hey Aleah, I totally get what you're saying—I loved this designer purse, but my parents said it was too expensive. I was so bummed! Try showing your parents how well you take care of your things and they may be more inclined to splurge on one item for your birthday, for instance.

✿ Helpful Hint

Learn to accessorize like a pro! The right belt, bracelet, or earrings can turn a basic outfit into a fashion statement. And if you want to spend money on trendy items, spend it on accessories. They are less expensive than clothes, and more versatile. Plus, it's fun to wear clunky bracelets, hoop earrings, and head scarves once in awhile. Just don't wear them all at once!

👁 Girl to Girl

Every girl should own one great pair of boots. All boot styles look fabulous with jeans, skirts, and dresses. They can dress an outfit up or down, and will definitely make a girl look cool— especially if she's wearing cowboy boots with a skirt!

★ Ashanti's Question: Size 14

I wear a size 14 and have trouble finding cool clothes that look good on me. I hate going shopping, because my mom always takes me to old-lady stores. Is there anywhere I can shop that has stylish clothes in bigger sizes?

Isabel Says

Hi sweetie! Don't freak out, there are a ton of cool stores and online sites for plus-sized girls. In fact, I just went shopping with my friend who is a size 16, and we had a great time! She found so many hot clothes and accessories. Since now the average American woman is a size 12 to 14, stores had to step it up and meet the demand.

Emily Says

Ashanti, our fashion expert Wendy McGill says that some great stores to find cool clothes in larger sizes are Torrid, Old Navy, Fashion Bug, and The Gap. And don't forget Target! There are also tons of trendy online stores, like www.alight.com and www. bandlu.com. When all else fails, buy simple clothes and complement them with stylish accessories and cute shoes.

Isabel Says

Wendy also mentioned that all girls can tame problem areas by wearing body shapers. These will slim bellies, butts, and hips to create smooth lines beneath your clothes.

✿ Helpful Hint

Do you know why celebs' clothes always fit perfectly? They go to a tailor! The fact is, clothes are mass-produced from cookie-cutter patterns, and don't fit everyone. But you can make your clothes look as if they were made for you by getting them tailored. If the dress you adore fits perfectly in some spots but not others, take to it a seamstress and have it custom-fit for your body.

Did You Know?

Having a shopping strategy before you hit the mall prevents overspending. Go with a budget, and stick to it. Avoid wasting your money by vowing to never buy anything unless you love it. Finally, never buy anything out of desperation!

✿ Fashion ....

Tips and Advice from Beauty Expert Wendy McGill

A lot of girls forget that fashion is supposed to be fun. Clothes and accessories are not just functional—they offer young women a way to express themselves. In fact, fashion is one way to be many different people all at the same time. You can be preppy one day and Goth the next. And in between these extremes are a million ways to create a visual presentation of who you are. Your style will always be evolving, and that is part of what is satisfying about building a wardrobe.

What is also interesting about fashion is that even when girls try a new look every few months, there are some core choices that appear over and over. These recurring fashion themes form a person's style. It's truly a delight to watch this process unfold!

Let your style take shape over time, and don't be in such a hurry to look like everyone else. It's the girls who dress uniquely that end up setting the trends.

Wrapping It Up

We've learned to stay on top of what's in and what's out. But we also know how to spot a bad, short-term fad—hello, thongs sticking out of your jeans?! Ick.

Know what looks good on you. This includes learning what colors work with your skin and hair. For example, some girls look washed out in black, but others look like rockstars! ★

Body Hygiene

Sugar and spice and everything nice...

Once puberty hits, there are so many things a girl has to deal with! And I'm talking about changes that are in addition to the regular stuff like periods and boobs. Around this time, many of us have to get braces, glasses, or retainers, which can be a downer.

❀ Body Hygiene ....

★ Emily's Perspective

I t's not all bad—we also get to paint our nails and get our ears pierced! These are really fun milestones that girls everywhere look forward to.

But some of the stuff we have to deal with can really make you cringe! One of the most embarrassing changes we face during puberty is developing weird body odors in super-private places. Ew! Smelling like a bag of onions after gym class is social suicide, so it must be avoided at all costs. This means taking showers, wearing deodorant, and changing our clothes often or dressing in layers. You may also start wearing perfume, but don't think this is a substitute for good hygiene!

★ Isabel's Perspective

T hat's a great point, sis. Perfume does not substitute for a shower after a soccer game! ☺

During puberty, there are some areas we need to start thinking more about, like the skin on our faces. Of course we all wash our faces in the morning, but how many of us also wash before going to bed? And I bet most of you don't wash your necks, shoulders, or backs. Well, get scrubbing girls because oils build up there too, and can cause nasty breakouts and "backne." Sick!

We also need to remember to wash our feet—even between our toes—because unfortunately, foot odor comes with the whole puberty package. Other areas you might not think to wash are behind your ears and knees. Seriously! Sweat covers all of you and can really make you stink. Also, wearing the same shirt to softball practice without washing it will definitely alert the team that your hygiene habits need work.

Having excellent body hygiene is a lot more than washing your hands after you use the bathroom! It's making sure your entire body is squeaky clean and smelling great.

Body Odors

"What soap is to the body, laughter is to the soul."
~ Yiddish Proverb

⚘ Helpful Hint

If you wear polyester and rayon shirts, wear a little cotton tank top underneath your clothes. Cotton fibers absorb sweat and let your skin breathe, which means less stink. So, go all-cotton for a natural way to limit your new smells. This is especially true for underwear!

And since stinky feet also come with the onset of puberty, invest in lots of cotton socks.

★ The Scoop

Body odors are a fact of life that we all wish we could forget! But since we can't, we might as well get a handle on them by understanding where they come from.

The first place you might notice a new smell is your armpits. Once puberty begins, sweat glands in your armpits become active. They pump out a mixture of sweat and chemicals that causes an unpleasant smell. Underarm odor may smell sickly sweet, or like garlic and onions. It depends on your body's particular chemistry and your diet.

Thanks to puberty and the changes it brings, your vagina may also have a new smell. Practicing good hygiene by bathing daily with a mild cleanser will prevent odors from becoming overpowering. However, some odor is normal and products like sprays, douches, and creams that promise to eliminate vaginal odors should always be avoided!

❁ Body Odors ....

★ Kiki's Question: Deodorant?

I sweat a lot, and lately I've been getting pit stains on my t-shirts. It is really embarrassing, but what's worse is that I also have serious B.O.! One of my friends said I should wear deodorant, but there are so many kinds. How do I know what kind to get?

Emily Says

Oh, I know Kiki—I sweat so much during soccer! Luckily, you can deal with this problem pretty easily by understanding what deodorants do. Antiperspirants prevent you from sweating. If you sweat a lot, this is the right choice. Deodorants, on the other hand, keep you from getting all smelly. It sounds like you have issues with both sweating and odor, so you should look for a product that does both.

❀ Helpful Hint

Your diet may stink! Caffeine, spicy foods, and meat increase perspiration. This doesn't mean you should avoid these treats, but limiting your consumption may reduce sweating. Also, avoid onions and garlic since they increase the B.O. factor.

☞ Expert's Point of View

Tips and Advice from Dr. Stuart Cohen

Body odor is a natural part of puberty and not a cause for concern. However, if frequent bathing and over-the-counter deodorants don't work, see your doctor. In some rare cases, severe body odor is a sign of a bacterial infection.

Wrapping It Up

Thanks to about a million different products, girls don't have to be stinky. Just shower every day, wear deodorant, and change your clothes daily. But seriously, avoid the temptation to mask stink with perfumes, because girls who do that end up smelling like grandmas! Gross! ★

Skin Care

"She's beautiful, and therefore to be woo'd.
She is a woman, therefore to be won."
~ William Shakespeare

★ The Scoop

Your skin is your body's largest organ. It is also your defense system against injury, infection, and temperature change. It protects your internal organs from sun damage and helps rid you of toxins through perspiration. Skin is also your connection to touch, and the way it forms over your bones gives you your unique appearance. With such important jobs, your skin needs to be cared for on a daily basis!

Getting into a skincare groove is easy and doesn't have to take more than 10 minutes a day. Start by using a gentle cleanser to keep your skin free of bacteria and pollutants. Moisturize dry areas—particularly your face, hands, elbows, knees, and feet—and get in the habit of wearing sunscreen every day. You will be so glad you used moisturizer and sunscreen when you are older, as dry, sun-exposed skin is the number one cause of wrinkles. The sooner you start caring for your skin, the better you'll hold up as the years go by.

❀ Helpful Hint

The secret to beautiful, glowing skin is water! Drinking 6 to 8 glasses of water each day will keep you hydrated, and hydration is the best way to have great-looking skin that stays soft. Staying hydrated prevents skin from drying out and flushes harmful toxins out of your body when you pee.

Another way to use water to keep skin moist is by using a humidifier while you sleep.

★ Emani's Question: Bumps

I started getting these ugly little bumps on my fingers a few months ago. They're gross and it seems like whenever I scratch one away a bunch more appear in that spot! What the heck are these things and what can I do to get rid of them?

Isabel Says

Ugh, it sounds like you've got warts! Dermatologist Dr. Fitzpatrick says you can get warts from touching someone else who has them. In other words, warts are contagious. Luckily, they can be treated. Start by putting an over-the-counter cream with salicylic acid on them. If they don't go away, your doc may freeze them using liquid nitrogen (cool!) or remove them by cutting them off or burning them (ouch!).

🌼 Did You Know?

Cold sores are caused by the HSV-1 virus, which is very contagious. So don't share lip balms or drink from others' cups. Though they can be painful and look gross, most cold sores will go away on their own within about 10 days.

👉 Expert's Point of View

Tips and Advice from Dr. Richard Fitzpatrick

Smart food choices help skin look great. Eating cantaloupe, carrots, sweet potatoes, spinach, blueberries, nuts, and beans protects skin from UV rays and helps it to heal faster. Also, foods like asparagus help skin retain elasticity.

Wrapping It Up

Taking care of your skin doesn't have to be time-consuming and is seriously worth it. Doing little things for your skin now will totally pay off in the long run. For instance, our aunt is 50 but looks really young because she started taking care of her skin when she was about our age. ★

Teeth

"I've never seen a smiling face that was not beautiful."
~ Author Unknown

Helpful Hint

To keep your teeth healthy and strong, limit the amount of sugar in your diet. When left to sit on your teeth, sugar turns acidic and wears away enamel.

Sugar also makes your teeth susceptible to plaque and cavities. It is especially important to cut out sugary beverages, such as soda, since just 1 can of non-diet soda contains up to 10 teaspoons of sugar!

★ The Scoop

Appear cool and confident each time you flash your pearly whites by practicing excellent oral hygiene.

The most important tool in your repetoire is your toothbrush. Brushing your teeth for 3 minutes twice a day is the most effective way to remove bacteria and plaque from your tooth enamel. Enamel protects the inner, soft part of your teeth, called the pulp. Using soft bristles to brush your teeth prevents erosion of the enamel, which is a good thing, because the pulp it protects contains nerves, which send pain signals to your brain. If you've ever had a cavity, you know what I mean! So, brush to avoid pain and visit your dentist regularly.

Another way to keep your teeth healthy and pain-free is to floss once a day. Flossing daily dislodges muck and reduces your risk for cavities. Plus, it keeps your breath fresh, which is important should you find yourself kissing someone! LOL!

★ Abbey's Question: Braces

My dentist told me to see an orthodontist to find out if I need braces. I'm not sure I want braces, though. They look like they hurt and some kids have to wear them for forever! How do braces work and how long would I have to wear them?

Emily Says

I have braces, and they're totally not a big deal. So don't be scared, Abbey! Braces work by putting pressure on your teeth to make them straight. Braces are actually brackets that are bonded to each tooth and connected by a wire. About once a month, your orthodontist will tighten the wire, which forces your teeth to move a little straighter. Your mouth will be sore for a few days, but you get used to it. What do you think, Isabel? You had 'em too... .

Isabel Says

Yep, and I know braces can feel like they take forever, but they have to work slowly so you're not dying from the pain of wrenching your teeth. But really, you'll only have them for about 2 years, which is a small price to pay for a gorgeous smile.

They shouldn't hurt too much day to day, but if your braces cut your mouth, you should ask for orthodontic wax. This coats the brackets and lets them slide along soft tissue inside your mouth.

⚙ Helpful Hint

After your braces are removed, you will be fitted for a retainer. Wearing a retainer helps your mouth "retain" all of the work braces did to your teeth and gums. Retainers are nearly invisible to other people. They are first worn for most of the day, and then only at night.

🥚 Did You Know?

If your permanent teeth are in and your case is not severe, Invisalign trays may work for you, instead of metal braces. Invisalign consists of plastic aligners that you switch out every 2 weeks. Each aligner is made just for you and will gradually shift your teeth into place. Invisalign works just like braces but is barely noticeable! Ask your dentist if Invisalign is an option.

★ Kiki's Question: Drilling

I just found out I have to have 2 cavities filled, and I'm freaking out! I could hear a drill in the other room and it sounded horrible! Do I have to get my cavities filled? Can't I just brush more often instead?

Isabel Says

Kiki, I'll give you the bad news first—you do have to get those cavities filled. My dentist, Dr. Hirsh, says that cavities form holes in your teeth. If you don't get cavities fixed, they cause nasty things like severe root pain, infections, and even bone loss.

So, since we both know you don't want any of that to happen, you're going to have to suck it up and face the drill. Which brings me to the good news: you won't feel it! Your dentist will numb your gums with a gel and then inject an anesthetic near your tooth so you won't feel a thing.

Emily Says

After you get your cavities filled, be sure to brush and floss regularly to avoid getting another one.

Even though you're brushing and flossing, Dr. Hirsh says to have your teeth professionally cleaned twice a year (or you may step this up to 4 times a year if you have braces). Dentists can clean down where your toothbrush can't!

✿ Helpful Hint

You can do something about gross bad breath! When brushing and flossing your teeth, don't forget to brush your tongue. Think of all the muck that gets absorbed in the thousands of taste buds that coat your tongue! Brushing your tongue and using mouthwash 1 or 2 times a day will give you fresh breath. This will give you confidence during close encounters of any kind.

Girl to Girl

If you're on the go and don't have time to brush, swish some water around inside your mouth after drinking soda or juice, then spit it out. This will at least rinse sugar and stain-causing liquid off your teeth until you can get home and brush.

❧ Teeth...

Tips and Advice from Dr. Gary Hirsh

The best advice I can offer (besides brushing regularly, of course) is to get at least 1,300 milligrams of calcium every day until you turn 18.

Research shows that calcium plays a big role in having strong, healthy teeth and gums. Consider that your bone mass—which includes teeth, since teeth are bone—is at its peak around age 20. As you get older, your bones and teeth become weaker and more prone to breakage. So, having a strong foundation is key for long-term dental and skeletal health.

It is best to get calcium from foods such as low-fat dairy products, dark green vegetables, nuts, and fortified cereals and juices. Also, watch your sugar intake—and not just candy and soda, but fruits and juices, too. These have tons of sugar and can hurt your teeth. You should not avoid eating fruit, but definitely brush soon after chomping on that apple.

Wrapping It Up

There's no need to add "smile phobia" to our list of insecurities. Who wants to worry that they have green stuff in their teeth, or gnarly onion breath? Not us. Plus, girls take a lot of pictures, so we all want pretty, white smiles.

Having a great smile is easy. We like to carry toothbrushes in our bags to brush our teeth after we eat. Just a quick brush and we feel so much cleaner! ★

Eyes

"The best and most beautiful things in the world cannot be seen or even touched. They must be felt with the heart."
~ Helen Keller

🌷 Helpful Hint

One way to keep your vision young is to eat foods rich in zinc, vitamins C and E, and beta-carotene. These vitamins and minerals have been shown to slow age-related vision loss over time. So, ask your mom to stock your kitchen with whole grains, yogurt, leafy greens, and yellow and orange fruits and vegetables. This way, you can make every meal look like a rainbow, which promotes healthy eyes.

★ The Scoop

Thankfully, eye care is a cinch compared to the rest of puberty. While you do need to protect your eyes, there is very little effort involved in having 20/20 vision.

You might be thinking, "How do I know if I have 20/20 vision?" Your vision is assigned a number based on a system devised back in 1863 that depends on how well you read a particular line on an eye chart from 20 feet away. If you can read the line labeled 20, you have 20/20 vision. If you are only able to read the first several lines, you may have 20/40 or 20/60 vision. This means you read lines from 20 feet that other people can see from 40 or 60 feet away. Got it?

The only way to find out your vision number is to have an annual eye exam. This is a short, painless visit that is valuable for detecting vision problems early enough to correct them. No sweat!

✿ Eyes ....

★ Marie's Question: Glasses

I'm so bummed—I just found out I have to wear glasses. My doctor said I'm nearsighted, and I don't even know what that means! I'm trying not to be a baby about it, but it seems like it will be seriously annoying to wear glasses all the time. Do I really have to wear them?!

Emily Says

OK Marie, Dr. Cohen says that being nearsighted means you can see stuff that is close up but objects that are far away look blurry. It's a common thing—in fact, 160 million people in America wear "corrective lenses," so you're not alone! And don't worry, glasses don't have to cramp your style. Get a cute, edgy pair and make them an accessory and part of your personal style!

✿ Helpful Hint

Contact lenses are an alternative to glasses that are simple, as well as compact and portable. You can try soft lenses, which are flexible and easy to get used to wearing, or gas-permeable lenses, which allow more oxygen to reach the eyes.

👉 Expert's Point of View

Tips and Advice from Dr. Stuart Cohen

Your parents may warn you that reading in dim light will damage your vision. However, this is a big eye-care myth! Although dim light won't damage your eyes, it will cause them to get tired faster, which cuts into your study time.

Wrapping It Up

Eyes are just another thing you can accessorize! Glasses come in all shapes and colors, and you can even get designer frames, if you can convince your mom that you'll take care of them! Or if you wear contacts, experiment with different colors or a little mascara to bring out your eyes! ★

Nails

"Hold a true friend with both hands."
~ Anonymous

⚘ Helpful Hint

Use a soft brush to scrub beneath your nails. This removes dirt that may contain bacteria. Always dry your nails after washing your hands to prevent fungus.

Also, apply cream with "urea," "phospholipids," or "lactic acid" to your cuticles (the skin at the base of your nails). These ingredients prevent the skin around your nails from drying out or cracking.

★ The Scoop

Pretty up your nails by keeping them filed and clean! It's really that simple. Of course, we also love to use nail polish to create a look. Dark polish is really cool, but you'll want to keep nails short and rounded. Longer nails are pretty in French manicures or light colors. Nail polish is also an easy (and cheap) way to experiment with a seasonal trend. Just don't let the polish chip and peel and get all gross. Remove nail polish about once a week and reapply.

If colored polish isn't your thing, you can protect your nails and encourage them to grow strong by coating them with a nourishing clear polish. But even clear polish needs maintenance—remove and reapply it once a week to avoid ending up with yellow nail beds.

Your fingernails give important clues about your overall health. Eating a balanced diet rich in calcium, vegetables, lean meats, and healthy fats will help them stay smooth and strong.

❀ Nails ....

★ Ashanti's Question: Hangnails

I keep getting these seriously painful hangnails. They make my fingertips sore, and it stings when I wash dishes or get lemon juice on them. I try to bite them off so they are too short to get caught on anything, but they kill! What can I do to get rid of this problem?

Isabel Says

That's your first problem Ashanti—stop biting your hangnails! It's seriously gross and unsanitary. Paint nasty-flavored polish on your nails to stop you from biting them. Beauty expert Wendy McGill also says to invest in a nail clipper to trim hangnails. Finally, since hangnails are usually caused by dry skin, keep your hands moisturized by wearing gloves with lotion in them to bed.

🌱 Helpful Hint

Leave great-looking nails to the professionals and use your allowance to get a manicure and pedicure every now and then. This is a fun activity to do with your girlfriends. Head to the salon for a relaxing mini spa day!

👉 Expert's Point of View

Tips and Advice from Beauty Expert Wendy McGill

It takes 100 days for nails to grow just 1 centimeter! To help yours grow in nicely, don't bite them, moisturize your cuticles every day, wear nail-hardening polish, and file your nails in the shape you want them to grow.

Wrapping It Up

Pretty doesn't necessarily mean super-long. Fake nails can look scary, and it's so embarrassing if one falls off during school. Acrylic nails also ruin your real nail bed. Plus, they can get in the way of activities, like playing music. If you are dying to try them, wait for a special occasion, like a dance. ★

Hands

"The best thing to hold onto in life is each other. "
~ Audrey Hepburn

★ The Scoop

We depend on our hands to do pretty much everything for us, but do you know how your hands actually work? Dr. Cohen says that we have 27 bones in each of our hands. These bones, 14 of which make up your fingers, allow your hands to grab, make a fist, and play musical instruments. Your hands also contain muscles and tendons that give them the strength and precision to help you become a surgeon, painter, or gymnast.

Our hands are also what most often physically connect us to other people through handshakes, hugs, and encouraging squeezes. If you've ever held hands with a guy, like while watching a movie or taking a walk, you know how awesome it can be just to press your hands together!

During puberty, hands can get really dry or really sweaty, so it's important to take care of them. After all, they're one of the most important parts of your body.

🌼 Helpful Hint

Keep your hands clean by washing them after you use the bathroom, before eating a meal, after petting an animal, after playing sports, and after touching shopping carts.

Indeed, a recent study proved that shopping cart handles can carry more bacteria than public restrooms! Sick! Squash germs with hand sanitizer and soap!

❀ Hands ....

★ May Ling's Question: Dry Hands

My hands are so dry! I put lotion on after I take a shower, but it feels like they suck it up in 2 seconds and then are dry again. But super-moisturizing lotions are greasy, and I don't like the way they feel. How can I keep my hands from drying out without having to use a heavy cream?

Emily Says

Ew, I hate goopy lotions, too! But there are lots of ways to deal with alligator hands. One is by putting some Vaseline (gross, I know, but keep reading!) on your hands right before bed and wear gloves while you sleep. This adds major moisture to dry skin. Or, carry a small, non-greasy lotion in your purse for quick and convenient relief after you wash your hands.

⚓ Helpful Hint

If you work with your hands or play certain sports, you might build up a tough layer of skin called a callus. Soak calluses in warm water and use a pumice stone to gently scrub away the buildup of dead skin.

☞ Expert's Point of View

Tips and Advice from Dr. Stuart Cohen

While it is true that knuckle cracking is not the best thing to do with your hands, since it stresses your joints, know that this habit does not cause arthritis. This is an old wives tale started by moms who were squeamish about this behavior.

Wrapping It Up

One of the grossest things a girl can do with her hands is crack her knuckles. Not only does it sound terrible, but it looks freaky. Plus, that popping sound happens because you push your bone out of its joint, which isn't good. So, stretch your fingers, but leave your bones in place, please! ★

Feet

*"Keep your eyes on the stars,
and your feet on the ground."
~ Theodore Roosevelt*

✿ Helpful Hint

Prevent athlete's foot by always wearing flip-flops in public showers because this gross condition is caused by a contagious fungus. Yuck! Also, always dry them completely and allow your feet to be exposed to the air for awhile.

When you wear shoes, wear cotton or wool socks because they allow feet to breathe and absorb moisture.

★ The Scoop

Put your best foot forward by keeping your feet clean, well-groomed, and beautiful!

Think about how much your feet do for you every day. For example, they carry your entire weight (plus backpacks, groceries, and books) from here to there. Yet you probably don't give them a second thought except to wash them in the shower. Well, it's time to change the way you view your feet.

One of the best ways you can care for your feet is to wear the right shoes. Shoes that fit properly should not be too snug or loose. They should be supportive, have a low heel, and let your feet breathe. Pair your shoes to your activity. This means wearing cleats when you play soccer and running shoes when you jog or exercise.

Truly, our feet do a ton for us. Sit back, relax, and put your feet up while you read on.

Feet..

★ Emani's Question: Stinky Feet

Every time I have to take my shoes off in front of other people I get so embarrassed, because my feet stink so badly! I thought it was my shoes, but I got a new pair and my feet still smell. I shower every day, so why do my feet reek like rotten onions?!

Isabel Says

Emani, your problem literally stinks! I am guessing this smell appeared out of the blue. You may have to wash your feet more than once a day and use baby powder to keep them dry. Also, try spraying disinfectant in your shoes. And definitely don't wear shoes without socks! Give your feet plenty of air time; keeping them dry and clean should cut the stench.

✿ Helpful Hint

Soften your feet by using a weekly foot scrub. Make your own by mixing almond oil with sugar or sea salt. Rub it into your heels and the outer edges of your feet. Let it sit for 2 minutes before rinsing your feet with warm water.

☞ Expert's Point of View

Tips and Advice from Dr. Stuart Cohen

Part of taking care of your feet means watching your step, especially when walking barefoot. Stepping on glass or a nail hurts and may require a painful tetanus shot or even stitches. Even a stubbed toe can leave an unsightly bruise.

Wrapping It Up

We love getting pedicures every now and then! It's not expensive (usually under $30) and makes you feel like a princess. Plus, pedicurists are professionals and know how to make feet super-soft and pretty. Even if you don't like nail polish, it's worth it for the foot and calf massage! ★

Ears

"Put your ear down close to your soul and listen hard."
~ Anne Sexton

⚓ Helpful Hint

Even though you may think it's gross, earwax has a few important jobs. For example, earwax keeps your ears moisturized. It keeps out infections and traps debris, preventing it from wiggling its way to your eardrum.

Be careful when cleaning earwax. Plunging cotton swabs deep into the ears may cause damage to the canal or even the eardrum.

★ The Scoop

Listen up! Your ears are more sensitive than you think. Your ears are part of a system that sends signals to your brain, letting you tell the difference between music, sirens, and rustling leaves.

Your ears are made up of 3 different parts. The outer ear is the part of the ear you can see. The middle ear contains the eardrum, which turns sound waves into vibrations. These vibrations travel along 3 tiny bones from your middle ear to your inner ear. When vibrations reach the inner ear, they cause teeny-tiny hairs to move, which sends a message to your brain that gets recognized as a dog barking or a horn honking! Pretty cool, huh.

What's not cool is that, over time, your hearing can become damaged, so you have to protect your ears from loud noises. Turn the music down and don't sit too close to the speakers at concerts. Your hearing depends on it!

✿ Ears ···

⚓ Helpful Hint

When you fly on an airplane the cabin pressure causes your ears to feel clogged and like you need to "pop" them. This is really uncomfortable, but you should be able to control it by yawning, chewing gum, or swallowing.

★ Katie's Question: Pierced Ears

I want to get my ears pierced, but I'm scared. Is there any way to do it that doesn't hurt? And if I go through with it, how long will it hurt and how do I make sure I don't get an infection?

Emily Says

I got my ears pierced and, yeah, it hurts for a few seconds, but it isn't as bad as you think. Most places use a piercing gun, which gets the piercing part over with really fast. Once the studs are in you'll need to wash your ear lobes with warm water, apply rubbing alcohol, and turn the studs frequently so they don't get crusty. Although it's tempting, don't take the earrings out for 6 to 8 weeks, because the holes can close up. And then you'll have to get them pierced all over again!

👉 Expert's Point of View

Tips and Advice from Dr. Stuart Cohen

Ear infections are painful and are caused by trapped water in the ear canal. Whenever you get out of the pool or ocean, shake excess water out of your ears and dry them thoroughly!

Wrapping It Up

We used to think hearing tests were boring and stupid. But Dr. Cohen made it clear that these tests help detect scary impairments. If problems go unnoticed, speech and learning problems can develop. Now we take hearing tests seriously—this is how doctors tell if there's a problem! ★

Puberty

We're in this together!

When our mom told us that going through puberty meant we would break out, bleed once a month, get cramps, have mood swings, develop breasts, have to wear a bra, grow hair in crazy places, gain weight, and cry for no reason, we nearly passed out!

❀ Puberty ....

★ Isabel's Perspective

Trust me, I begged her to not make me go through it. I tried to find a way around the whole thing. I thought maybe I could go from being a kid straight into adulthood without having to go through puberty. But I finally learned that it happens to all girls. I was no exception.

Then, one of my girlfriends, who is 17, told me, "Going through puberty makes you smarter, because you have to learn so much so fast." She was totally right! Once my body started changing, I learned all kinds of stuff about biology, chemistry, and even a few things about relationships, emotions, and love.

★ Emily's Perspective

Watching Isabel completely freak out (we thought she was going crazy), made me realize that I wasn't the only girl who was feeling scared about going through puberty. That was a huge step toward accepting, even loving, the changes beginning to happen to my body. Of course, it's easy to forget you are not alone, because what's happening to our bodies is so private. We grow hair on our vaginas and under our arms and develop boobs! Who wants to talk about THAT stuff?! I know I didn't at first. I felt embarrassed, like a total freak! But after awhile, I got more comfortable talking to my mom, my sister, my older friends, and my doctors about this stuff—their perspectives totally helped me feel less alone.

Definitely do yourself a favor and find 1 or 2 older girls or women to talk to—your mom, your friends, or a trusted teacher—because no one should have to go through puberty alone!

Acne

*"Turn your face to the sun
and the shadows fall behind you."
~ Maori Proverb*

★ The Scoop

During puberty, your body releases hormones that tell the oil glands in your face, neck, chest, and back to wake up! These oil glands make your skin greasy, which traps bacteria and pollution. All this junk clogs your pores, which causes acne—both whiteheads and blackheads.

You're probably thinking, "It's not fair! My skin was flawless a minute ago!" But don't worry, you aren't alone. According to the American Academy of Dermatology, almost 100 percent of teens break out. And 40 percent have severe enough breakouts to need medical help. For most girls, though, breakouts taper off around 5 to 10 years after the onset of puberty. So, you can expect clear skin again in your 20s!

Remember, having a few breakouts doesn't mean you have to become a full-fledged crater face. You can contain zits before they become a total disaster!

❀ Girl to Girl

Breakouts are huge bummers, but don't squeeze, pop, or pick at zits. This makes skin really irritated and usually makes the pimple redder, crusty, and more noticeable. Plus, picking and popping spreads bacteria and encourages more breakouts!

Besides, if you pop a zit, like at school, and it starts to bleed, it's really nasty.

Acne

✦ Ashanti's Question: Pizza Face

I have pretty bad breakouts about once a month. My skin starts to feel extra greasy and my whole face turns into one giant zit factory! Why does this keep happening? Is it because of all the pizza I eat?

Isabel Says

Don't worry girl, our dermatologist Dr. Fitzpatrick says breakouts don't have anything to do with eating chocolate or greasy food like pizza. Just don't touch your face if you have greasy, dirty hands!

It sounds like you're getting breakouts right before your period. Dr. Fitzpatrick says this is because of "hormone surges." Ugh! Pimples are just, like, the icing on the cake of a really hard week!

Emily Says

I just started getting my period, Ashanti, and I totally know how you feel. Before my period I make sure to keep my hair out of my face. Oh, and you should wash your face both in the morning and before bed, since oils really tend to build up throughout the day and while you're asleep.

Isabel Says

One last thing Ashanti—drink plenty of water. That can help reduce breakouts, too.

❀ Helpful Hint

Since acne is caused by oil buildup in your pores, you really want to avoid adding more oil to problem areas. For example, if your forehead breaks out a lot, don't let your hair hang in your face—especially if you use gel or hairspray to style your bangs. This will only aggravate skin and cause it to break out more.

👁 Girl to Girl

You don't want use the same lotion on your face that you do for your body. Body lotion is usually heavier and will be too greasy for your face. Also, most body lotions don't provide sun protection, which you need every day. Choose an oil-free moisturizer with SPF that is specifically for the face.

★ Abbey's Question: Body Breakouts

This is so gross to admit, but after every volleyball game, I get pimples on my chest and back, especially right where my sports bra straps are. I'm too embarrassed to wear strappy tank tops now! What can I do to stop breaking out on my body?

Emily Says

Ugh! I hate when I get "backne" after a soccer game. It's so frustrating. Dr. Fitzpatrick suggested that I wear loose-fitting shirts when I can, since tight clothing can trap dirt in your skin. I like "dry-fit" tops, which soak up sweat and keep it off your skin.

Isabel Says

Abbey, the skin on your back is tougher than the skin on your face or chest, so it might take a more hardcore cleanser. Luckily, there are some good cleansers designed specifically for "backne," so grab one the next time you go grocery shopping.

Emily Says

Good point Isabel. Abbey, your chest is more sensitive, so don't over-scrub it. Just use your regular facial cleanser and be sure to shower after your volleyball games. Keeping fresh and clean will prevent body breakouts from popping up in the first place.

❁ Girl to Girl

If acne makes you feel embarrassed, ashamed, or upset, it is time to ask your parents to see a dermatologist. There is no reason to allow breakouts to control your happiness or social life. Once you start the right treatment, you should see positive results within a few weeks.

Treatments include office visits, topical creams, and possibly oral medication. Treatment takes time, so be patient and give medications time to do their jobs.

Fun Fact

Some pimple creams are flesh-colored, which is great, because they zap zits and cover them up without causing flare-ups.

❀ Acne  ....

Tips and Advice from Dr. Richard Fitzpatrick

What's the truth about acne? Well, first, there is virtually no evidence to support the claim that sweets or greasy foods cause acne. Second, acne is not necessarily caused by poor hygiene, though additional oil from greasy hair and fingers can cause breakouts to become irritated. Third, stress can actually aggravate acne. Stress is an inflammatory response in the body and causes the adrenal glands to go into overdrive, leading to breakouts.

However, know that you are not powerless over pimples. There are many over-the-counter creams that are very effective. And dermatological treatment is an excellent way to manage mild to severe bouts of acne.

Finally, if you find yourself in the midst of an acne emergency, such as a huge pimple right before a school dance, see your dermatologist. He or she can use a cortisone injection to reduce the size and redness of a pimple in as little as 24 hours.

Wrapping It Up

Let's face it—pimples are ugly, they hurt, and they make kids feel bad about themselves. Our advice is to remember that we are all in the same boat. Every single teenager on the planet gets zits now and then. Seriously! No one is spared zits all together, so let's not be mean to each other about it. If we stick together and say, "Hey, pimples are a fact of life!" maybe girls would get less depressed about them. ★

Periods

"I love to see a young girl go out
and grab the world by the lapels."
~ Maya Angelou

★ The Scoop

First zits and body odor, and now periods! However, the arrival of your period is the main event for girls during puberty and signifies that you're really becoming a woman. Although this can be a confusing and scary time for us, it doesn't have to be. By learning what causes your body to menstruate once a month, you are taking an important step in learning how to care for your new body.

Periods are a nuisance, but they are a natural part of growing up. You might view puberty as laying the groundwork for later on—when you are older and ready for grown-up stuff like pregnancy.

Most girls get their first period between the ages of 9 and 16. Once you get your first period—called *menarche*—you have entered your childbearing years. This means that starting now, your ovaries will release an egg each month in a process called ovulation. The egg travels through your fallopian tubes toward your uterus. Meanwhile, your uterus develops a thick lining called an endometrium. This lining houses and nourishes the egg and would allow it to grow into a baby if sperm were present to fertilize it. When pregnancy occurs, women are without their periods for 9 months!

However, for the majority of your life, the egg will not be fertilized, and so your uterus sheds the endometrium, blood, and egg. These fluids exit your body through your vagina in a reddish-brown blood-and-fluid mixture that is called your period.

On average, your period will last about 5 days, although some may be as short as 2 days or as long as 7 days. Ovulation usually occurs 2 weeks before you get your period. These weeks are all part of what is called your menstrual cycle. Your monthly cycle may be set up so that you get your period every 28 days, which is the average for most girls. However, girls' periods might show up as early as every 20 days or as late as every 35 days. And many girls have irregular periods, sometimes skipping a month here and there—especially in the beginning. It just depends on your particular body's biological clock. However, if your period stays irregular for more than a few cycles, let your parents or doctor know.

Go With The Flow

Don't get caught off-guard by your first period! Know what to expect and what supplies you need. Now that you know why you get your period, the best way to deal with menstruation is to be prepared. After all, getting your period at school while wearing a white skirt would be awful! So, keep an eye on your cycle by keeping a period calendar. Tracking when you last got your period will help you predict when it will come again. When you think your period might be on its way, put some tampons or pads in your backpack, purse, or locker. It's best to always be ready, since your period may not be regular in the beginning. Plus, carrying extras lets you to come to the rescue should a friend find herself in need!

Periods ❀

★ Katie's Question: First Period Coming?

I'm so scared that I am going to get my period any day now! And when I do I will have no idea what to do! I live with my dad, and there's no way I can ask him about this stuff. What should I do and who should I ask? I don't even know how to use a pad or what to do with one once I'm done with it.

Isabel Says

Katie, if you think you are going to get your period soon then you probably are. I mean, doctors always tell us that we know our bodies best, right?

So, be ready! There are lots of ways to learn what to do—reading this book is a great first step! A good person to talk to is your school nurse. She will have supplies in her office in case you're surprised by your period when you're at school. And if you're too scared to talk to her, ask a friend to ask her mom to help.

Emily Says

Hey Katie! I started with pads until I got comfortable using tampons. Pads have a sticky bottom and little side flaps, which keep them in place in your underwear. When you're done with one, just fold it up, wrap some toilet paper around it, and toss it in the trash.

❀ Helpful Hint

The reason your breasts are sore before your period is because of hormones called estrogen and progesterone. These hormones circulate in your body, which causes tenderness in various places. Wearing a sports bra to bed can reduce breast tenderness. Other remedies include using a heating pad, soaking in a warm bath, and taking over-the-counter pain relievers.

❀ Girl to Girl

You might feel pretty bloated right before and during your period. Avoid eating salty foods because sodium will make you retain water. But drinking water dilutes sodium, so stay hydrated! Also, exercise will help you feel better, so get moving.

★ May Ling's Question: Tampons

I am way too embarrassed to ask my mom how to use tampons, but I want to try them. I like to swim a lot in the summer, and I obviously can't wear pads in the water. Help! How do I put a tampon in?

Isabel Says

Don't panic, May Ling! Tampons are easy to use once you get the hang of them.

First, either sit on the toilet or put one foot up on the bathtub. Hold the tampon in the same fingers you write with and make sure the string sticks out of the applicator. This part is embarrassing, but do it anyway: Open up your vaginal lips with your other hand and insert the tampon. Push it up and

❂ Helpful Hint

Toxic shock syndrome (TSS) is a rare but serious condition that can develop from using tampons. When used improperly tampons can introduce bacteria to your body that can lead to TSS. To avoid TSS, change your tampon every 4 to 8 hours. Use the smallest size tampon to handle your flow. Make sure your hands are clean when you insert a tampon, and never use tampons when you do not have your period.

Girl to Girl

Wear panty liners a few days before and after your period in case it shows up early or to catch spotting afterward. And don't stress—light spotting between periods is totally normal!

❂ Inserting a Tampon · · · · · · · · · · · · · ·

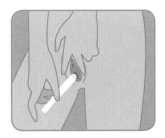

Step 1
Hold the plastic applicator between your thumb and middle finger (you will use your first finger to push the tampon in). Find a comfortable position—some girls like to stand with one foot up, such as on the edge of the bathtub, or sit down with knees spread.

Step 2
With the hand not holding the applicator, pull open the folds of skin around the vaginal opening. Position the rounded tip of the tampon (not the end with the string) against your vaginal opening.

stop once your hand touches your vagina. Then, push the the applicator all the way in. Congrats girl—it's in!

Remove the applicator, toss it in the trash, wash your hands, and you're in business.

Emily Says

Isabel makes it sound easy, but she was actually too squeamish to show me (thanks sis)! I was so freaked out to use tampons, but I figured it out with a little practice. Just relax or you'll tense up, which will make things even more difficult.

Start with a small size tampon. Practice a few times, and if you mess up, it's easy to start over.

Girl to Girl

Don't let the color of your period freak you out. It's completely normal for your period to be all shades of red and even brown. When blood is exposed to air, it oxidizes, or turns from red to brown—so when you have a fast-flowing, heavier period it will be brighter red. A lighter, slower period will look more brown in color because it is exposed to more air.

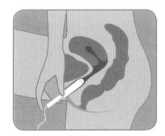

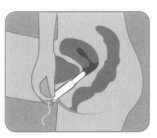

Step 3
The vagina slants at an angle, so you should slide the applicator in gently, tilting it at an upwards and backwards angle. It will help to stay relaxed when you ease the applicator in. Stop pushing when the fingers holding the applicator meet your body.

Step 4
Now that the applicator is inserted, use your first finger to push the bottom of the small tube completely up inside the big tube. This slides the tampon into your vagina, leaving the string outside your body. Then, simply pull out the plastic applicator, wrap it up, and throw it in the trash.

Fun Fact

Girls who spend a lot of time together often start getting their periods around the same time! The theory is that our bodies give off undetectable chemicals called pheromones that can make girlfriends', sisters', and roommates' periods synch up.

❁ Periods................

★ Ashanti's Question: Cramps!

I seriously have the worst cramps in the universe when I get my period. I can barely get out of bed, they're so painful! I've tried a bunch of over-the-counter pain relievers and nothing seems to do the trick. I end up staying home from school for like 2 days when I get my period. Is there anything that will get rid of really bad cramps so I don't have to miss so much school?

Emily Says

Cramps are such an unfair part of the whole period thing, aren't they? I'm really sorry you get such bad ones Ashanti, but there are ways to make it so you can still go to school. It's really important that girls know we don't have to be in pain.

For starters, talk to your doctor about prescription painkillers or muscle relaxers. Dr. Cohen also recommends using a heating pad for a half-hour when cramps are at their worst. Plus, even though you don't feel like it, exercise. It totally cuts down on the pain.

Isabel Says

Ashanti, Dr. Cohen also says that if you ever have sharp pains in your abdomen, soak more than 2 pads in an hour, or bleed for 10 days or more, see a doctor right away.

❁ Did Your Know?

Thanks to hormones, headaches often come with periods. Some are so bad that your eyes become sensitive to light, you see spots, and you feel nauseous. This type of headache is a migraine and will require medical intervention. For regular headaches, pain relievers plus lying down in a dark room with an ice pack on your head will help.

Fun Fact

In the 1930s, Dr. Earle Haas patented his version of the tampon, which included an applicator. When he was unable to get a company to buy his invention, he sold the rights to Gertrude Tenderich for $32,000. She went on to mass-produce them under the brand name Tampax!

★ Aleah's Question: Tampons & Virginity

A girl in my gym class said that if I use tampons I won't be a virgin anymore because they can break your hymen. I want to start using tampons on a regular basis but not if that's true!! Help!

Isabel Says

Don't worry Aleah—you can *definitely* use tampons and still be a virgin. In reality, virginity has to do with sexual intercourse and nothing to do with inserting a tampon.

Besides, you shouldn't stress so much about tearing your hymen. According to Dr. Cohen, your hymen is a just very thin layer of tissue that partially covers the opening to the vagina. He says it's so fragile that a lot of girls will naturally stretch or tear their hymens during sports or other physical activities.

Emily Says

So true, sis. Lots of girls start using tampons when they're pretty young because they play a sport or swim. I think tampons are great—once you get the hang of them, you can't feel them at all. They're actually comfortable! Of course, Aleah, using tampons is totally up to you, but it sounds like you're ready for them. So don't listen to that myth about tampons—now you know the truth!

✿ Girl to Girl

Some girls are afraid that a tampon will get lost inside them, but don't worry—the opening in the cervix is only big enough to let a small amount of menstrual blood through, not big enough for a tampon to go up into the cervix. When you insert a tampon, it will fit snugly between the walls of your vagina. When you're ready to remove it, just pull the string—and *voila!* ☺

🌰 Did You Know?

Tampons actually date back as far as ancient Greece and Egypt. Back then, they were made of many different materials, including wool, papyrus, cotton, sponges, and wood pulp. These days, they're made from cotton or rayon or a combo of both.

 Periods......................................

Expert's Point of View

Tips and Advice from Dr. Stuart Cohen

The week before your period you may feel like you are losing control over your emotions. Don't worry ladies, you are not crazy! You're just like millions of girls—3 out of 4 women, in fact—who suffer from premenstrual syndrome (PMS). Though no one knows exactly what causes PMS, doctors attribute it to changing hormone levels.

Usual symptoms of PMS include mood swings, food cravings, depression and bouts of crying, aches and pains, and acne. However, if your symptoms are severe enough to prevent you from engaging in normal activities, talk to your doctor. In some cases, PMS symptoms highlight underlying depression. This can make symptoms unmanageable and a doctor's treatment is required.

However, for the majority of girls, PMS is fleeting and manageable with rest, good nutrition, exercise, over-the-counter pain relievers—and patience!

Wrapping It Up

Girls, once you get past your first period, you will get used to it—we promise! What's weird is everyone considers you a woman, but inside you still feel like a kid. But what we've learned is that just because we have our periods now doesn't mean we can't still goof around and wrestle with our brother. Our bodies are definitely changing, but we still have a few years before we have to really grow up! ☺ ★

Breasts

"One is not born a woman, one becomes one."
~ Simone de Beauvoir

✿ Helpful Hint

Many girls' breasts develop so that one is smaller than the other. This is 100 percent normal, so don't feel weird if it happens to you! In fact, many times one side develops its breast bud up to 6 months before the other.

Your breasts will probably catch up to each other, but if there is a big size difference that bothers you, wear an insert in your bra to even out their appearance.

★ The Scoop

The first stage of breast development occurs before puberty begins when your chest is flat and there is little color in the nipple area.

The second stage starts at puberty when little breast buds form beneath both nipples. Also, the circles around your nipples—called *areolas*—will darken and spread.

The third stage is a continuation of the second—breasts get a bit larger, nipples stick out more, and areolas become darker.

The fourth stage of breast development is when a tiny mound rises out of the breast, though many girls skip this and go straight to the final stage.

In the fifth and final stage of development, breasts take on a round, full shape with darkened areolas and raised nipples. This stage is usually completed when a girl is about 17 years old.

✿ Breasts ....

✿ Girl to Girl

Have you noticed red lines on the sides of your breasts or hips? If so, you have stretch marks. Though they're not the prettiest body accent, they are common and harmless. Stretch marks are a side effect of your skin stretching as your body develops. While you can't get rid of them, you can make them less noticeable by moisturizing with cocoa butter.

Helpful Hint

Growing tissue causes skin to stretch, which can make your chest dry. To reduce itching and redness, put lotion on your breasts after you shower, while you are still damp, to lock in moisture. For particularly itchy skin, take lukewarm baths with a dash of olive oil in the water.

★ Katie's Question: Flat-chested

My boobs are so small, it's depressing. I'm too self-conscious to wear anything tight because it just makes it more obvious that I have no boobs! I don't get it, because my mom has pretty big boobs, and so does my sister. When are my boobs going to grow, and how can I tell how big they will be?

Emily Says

Aw Katie, I know exactly how you feel! Isabel has big boobs, so I figured I would too—but it hasn't happened so far! The thing is, it's impossible to predict, because your breast size is not based on your mom's or sister's size. But once you get your period, who knows how big they might get! My advice is to find a bra with a little bit of padding until you develop more. Also, empire-waist shirts and dresses can make your boobs look bigger.

Isabel Says

Here's the thing, Katie: Big boobs definitely aren't always better. I was a C cup in middle school and I was so miserable. Boys picked on me all the time and some girls were really nasty, too. I eventually learned to like being curvy, but lot of girls probably wish their boobs were smaller like yours.

Emily Says

In my opinion, small boobs are cute. I mean, models always have small chests!

★ Abbey's Question: Lumpy Breasts

My boobs are still pretty small, but they feel really lumpy! I know lumps can sometimes mean breast cancer, so I'm kinda freaked out. Should I tell my mom or my doctor?

Emily Says

Don't worry Abbey! Dr. Cohen says that most girls and women have some natural lumpiness in their breasts. So this is totally normal!

The most important thing, he says, is to do a Breast Self Exam, or BSE, often, so you are familiar with how your breasts feel normally. That way you will know if anything weird starts happening in the future.

Isabel Says

I had this exact same question, Abbey. My breasts get really lumpy, especially during my period. But now that I know it happens to most girls, I don't worry so much.

You're probably still too young to have to do frequent BSEs, but in a few years, you'll want to do one every month or so. Lumps you can move around, or a pebbly, grainy texture are normal, but if you notice a bump that seems harder or larger than the others, tell your doctor. It's always smart to get an expert's opinion.

⚙ Did You Know?

As your breasts develop, your nipples can be large and wide, short and spiky, flat, or even inverted. All of these types of nipples are normal. Also, it's possible that your areolas will be widespread across your breasts, have many small bumps, and even sprout hairs. It's best to leave bumps and hairs alone—they're just a part of your beautiful body!

🏈 Fun Fact

Before you beg mom and dad for breast implants, consider this: A study found that 40 percent of women who have this surgery end up with a serious complication within 3 years. Also, many women require more surgeries within 5 and 10 years.

❀ Breasts ....

👉 Expert's Point of View

Tips and Advice from Dr. Stuart Cohen

Start developing habits that promote healthy breasts now. Eating a diet rich in fruits and vegetables and low in fat provides your breasts with ammunition to ward off cancer.

In addition, get in the habit of examining your breasts regularly for abnormal lumps and bumps. Give yourself a breast exam in the shower. Raise your arm above your head and feel around your breast for anything suspicious.

You are also never too young to avoid habits that are damaging to breasts. One habit to avoid is smoking. Smoking within 5 years of getting your first period nearly doubles your risk of getting breast cancer as an adult! This is because your breast tissue is still developing and is easily damaged by toxins in cigarettes. Also, smoking depresses estrogen levels, which is bad for your developing body. So, give your breasts a fighting chance and stay away from cigarettes!

Wrapping It Up

If you ask us, girls spend too much time thinking about boob size. Seriously, some girls are obsessed with how big or small their boobs are! After awhile, you just have to accept your breasts for what they are—the right size for your particular body. And besides, getting good grades, looking cute, and having fun with our friends is way more important—and breast size has nothing to do with any of those things! ⭐

Bras

"Having a good boyfriend is like having a good bra, it's all about support!"
~ Anonymous

⚓ Helpful Hint

When you go bra shopping, your goal is to find a bra that fits, is comfortable, and gives the right amount of support. Understanding this is your first step! Your second step is to ask your mom, aunt, or sister to take you bra shopping.

Then, dive in and try on bras. Grab a bunch of different sizes and styles and see which ones fit and look the best.

★ The Scoop

Going from a t-shirt-only existence to having to wear a bra can be a big change. But choosing a bra doesn't have to be scary or embarrassing. You just need to learn the right style and fit for your particular size. Bras come in 6 basic styles: training bras, soft-cup, underwire, push-up, padded, and sports bras.

Most girls who are buying their first bra stick to training and sports bras. Training bras are perfect for preteens and girls whose breasts do not need much support. These are also designed for girls who do not yet fit in standard cup sizes. Another great option is the sports bra. This type of bra is very comfy and gives a little more support than a training bra.

The most important feature of any bra is that you are comfortable wearing it!

❁ Bras ....

★ Aleah's Question: Support

I'm at the point where I need a bra with more support than my training bra gives me. My sister and mom both wear underwire bras, but they look uncomfortable! How do I know what size and kind of bra to get next?

Isabel Says

Congrats Aleah—you've graduated out of your training bra! My mom told me to measure around your rib cage, just below your boobs, then add 5 to that measurement and round up to the next even number. This is the number portion of your size, such as 34. For cup size, you'll have to try different bras to find whether you're an A, B, C, D, etc. And don't worry, underwire bras are actually comfortable, supportive, and easy to get used to.

❁ Helpful Hint

When buying a bra, choose one that fits on the outermost hook. As the bra stretches over time, you can simply hook it on one of the inner eyes. This ensures a good fit for a longer period of time! A bra you wear often will keep it's shape for about a year.

👉 Expert's Point of View

Tips and Advice from Dr. Stuart Cohen

There is no reason to wear a bra to bed. However, it will benefit you to wear a sports bra at night if your breasts are sore due to menstruation or development. The additional support minimizes pain caused by movement during sleep.

Wrapping It Up

Don't worry about what bra every other girl is wearing. Girls our age don't really need push-up bras, for instance—who wants more attention on their boobs? But you don't want to squish your boobs flat either. Try on LOTS of bras to find ones that are flattering under all your clothes. ★

Hair Growth

"God created man before woman. But then you always make a rough draft before the final masterpiece."
~ Author Unknown

⚓ Helpful Hint

Sometimes, girls grow hair in areas more often seen on guys, like the chin, upper lip, and sides of the face. If this happens to you, do not shave with a razor! This will only make hairs that were light enough not to be noticed sprout up black and wiry when they grow back.

Instead, pluck with tweezers, wax them, or carefully bleach them with products designed for the face.

★ The Scoop

Hair "down there" and in other new places is a perfectly normal part of puberty, it just takes a little getting used to. If you are like most girls, one day you looked in the mirror and noticed darker, curly hair growing on your vagina. If so, this is one of the earliest signs that puberty has begun!

Hair grows in weird places during puberty due to hormones called *androgens*. Androgens also cause hair to grow under your arms and on your legs. This hair actually has a function; special hormones called *pheromones* cling to the hair. Humans have been using pheromones to attract mates since caveman times!

Body hair also protects sensitive areas from irritation and infection. However, it is OK to trim, shave, and pluck hair to look neat and groomed.

Hair Growth..................

★ Katie's Question: Bikini Blues

I've got all this hair that pokes out of my bathing suit. It's, like, a lot of hair! It goes almost all the way down to my knees. I didn't really care about it until someone made a joke. Now I want to get rid of it! What's the best way to go back to looking normal in a bathing suit?

Isabel Says

Isn't it weird how everything is normal one day and the next, you feel like a gorilla? The area you're talking about is your bikini line, Katie, and there are a couple of ways to deal with this. Although you can wax the area that runs along your bathing suit and down the insides of your thighs, this can be pretty painful. The best way to start is probably to shave.

Use a fresh razor and always shave in the direction that hair grows to reduce the chance of getting ingrown hairs, which are painful and look gross.

If you're not ready to shave or wax, try wearing board shorts; they look cute and hide extra hair. My sister loves them!

Emily Says

Board shorts are a good option, Katie! Really, choose what is most comfortable for you—not what other people say!

❀ Helpful Hint

Shaving your legs is easier if you do it after you've soaked in a warm bath or shower for awhile. This is because warm water makes skin softer and less prone to nicks, scrapes, and ingrown hairs.

For a smooth, clean shave, use shaving cream or gel rather than soap. When you are finished shaving, wait 20 minutes and put a light lotion on your legs to seal in moisture.

Girl to Girl

If having a uni-brow has got you down on your appearance, attack it with a pair of tweezers or have it waxed. But whatever you do, do not shave it! This area is very sensitive; plus, you don't want icky stubble!

Hair Growth

★ Emani's Question: Hair Trail

This is so humiliating, but all of a sudden I've got hair in some really weird places. Like, I have this long trail of hair that goes down from my belly button! And hair under my arms. I feel like I look like a boy. Is this normal, and what can I do to get rid of it?

Emily Says

Emani, you are totally normal, don't even worry about it! Puberty does weird things to girls, and one of the weirdest is how much hair we get, and where. Dr. Cohen says the hair under your arms is there to keep your skin from getting irritated. Shaving under your arms is really easy, and most American women do it.

Isabel Says

So true Emani—shaving your armpits is probably the easiest shave job you'll do! As for the hair under your belly button, it's sometimes called a "Happy Trail" (although I'm sure you're not happy about it). Turns out it's just an extension of your pubic hair. It's normal and common, so don't worry, you're not a boy! Try plucking dark hairs with tweezers.

FYI—teens should avoid depilatories, aka, chemicals that dissolve body hair—because they may cause allergic reactions or severe rashes.

🌼 Helpful Hint

Never shave your legs or armpits when they are dry! This will result in razor burn. Razor burn looks like a rash and may produce painful red bumps or really dry, itchy patches of skin. If you do get razor burn, try soothing products made with aloe vera gel or tea tree oil. Also, toss out your dull razor!

Girl to Girl

Waxing to remove hair can be kind of painful, because it involves ripping out hair with hot, sticky wax. But it's quick and will leave those areas hairless for 3 to 6 weeks! For it to work, hair must be at least ¼-inch long. Waxing kits are sold in drugstores, but have your mom help you, or visit a salon and seek out a pro.

❀ Hair Growth...............................

Tips and Advice from Dr. Stuart Cohen

Once you decide to remove underarm and leg hair, you will have to choose a method. With some practice you'll come through the experience without a scratch!

If you choose a razor, stand in a warm shower with plenty of shaving cream lathered in your armpits and on your legs. Raise your arm and shave from top to bottom of your armpit. Rinse well and inspect your work in the mirror. For legs, work your way up from the lower leg, and be especially careful around your ankle bones, shins, and knees. If you do nick yourself, try pressing an ice cube on the cut for 2 minutes, then dab on antibiotic ointment.

Another option is to use an electric razor, which can lessen nicks and cuts. These can also be used on dry skin, though you should not use one while wearing deodorant or while in the shower.

Wrapping It Up

Don't let body hair (or lack thereof) get you down. Especially since there are so many ways to deal with it! We both shave our armpits, legs, and bikini lines to get rid of dark hair. Now is also a great time to start plucking your eyebrows! We suggest asking your mom to take you to a professional the first time. A pro can help shape your brows perfectly, so you can just touch them up with tweezers. Simple! ★

Stomach

"A chuckle comes from the belly; but a good laugh bursts forth from the soul, overflows, and bubbles all around."
~ Carolyn Birmingham

★ The Scoop

The last thing a girl wants is to get thicker around the middle, but this is just another in a long list of changes we can expect during puberty. Like other parts of puberty, these changes are to prepare our bodies for later in life, when we are ready to have babies.

As your belly changes shape, you may get stretch marks on your stomach and hips. Though many girls think they're ugly, stretch marks are just a normal part of growing up.

The good news is none of these body changes are painful. Some components of puberty will be uncomfortable in your stomach area, however. When you get your period, for example, you may have stomach cramps, bloating, gas, and some nausea. Although these cause discomfort, they are normal side effects of menstruation. These symptoms can be managed by taking pain relievers and antacids, as well as by using a heating pad.

❀ Girl to Girl

Many girls experience nausea and diarrhea during their periods. This is normal, but uncomfortable. If your stomach gets upset when you get your period, avoid eating greasy, high-fat foods, because these can increase symptoms.

Not bingeing on junk food will also pay off by reducing bloating, gas, and general feelings of ickiness that often accompany your period.

★ Haley's Question: Constipation

I never had this problem before, but sometimes I can't go number 2! This makes me feel fat, bloated, and uncomfortable. Also, when this happens my clothes don't fit and I get bad stomach aches. How can I keep my body from getting so "backed up"?

Emily Says

Aw, that's the worst Haley! Dr. Cohen told me the best way to prevent constipation is to eat lots of fiber. For example, pears, apples, and whole grains like brown rice are great food choices that will help keep you "regular." He also said that drinking lots of water—like 6 to 8 glasses—will keep your poop soft so that it doesn't plug up your insides.

🌼 Helpful Hint

Keeping stomach muscles strong prevents lower back pain when you play sports or lift heavy objects. Flabby stomach muscles force the lower back to work harder to keep your body upright. So add abdominal crunches to your daily exercise routine.

☞ Expert's Point of View

Tips and Advice from Dr. Stuart Cohen

Girls between the ages of 10 and 14 will gain anywhere from 15 to 55 pounds during puberty. It may be hard to imagine, but most of that weight will end up in your midsection, including your stomach, hips, buttocks, and thighs.

Wrapping It Up

A lot of us go from stick-skinny to more curvy during puberty, which can be tough when the whole world is obsessed with being tiny. But becoming more developed is actually kinda cool and can give a girl new confidence in her body. And FYI—skinny or curvy, guys love confident girls! ★

Body Changes

"The question isn't who's going to let me;
it's who is going to stop me."
~ Ayn Rand

🌸 Helpful Hint

During your growth spurt, think twice before making expensive clothing purchases. You'll probably just outgrow that outfit in a few weeks or months. It really happens that fast!

Luckily, shopping for vintage or secondhand clothing has become fashionable and fun. As long as you look cute and spend your hard-earned babysitting bucks wisely, you'll feel great.

★ The Scoop

By the time you get through puberty, your entire body will look different! Since girls usually start puberty earlier than boys, they also hit their growth spurts sooner. For girls, our growth spurt usually hits within 1 to 2 years of developing breast buds. Whenever your growth spurt hits, know that it will be a totally significant change—but one you should embrace! A growth spurt is a big deal because it is the beginning of many physical changes to come—the biggest one, duh, is getting a lot taller.

Growing taller before boys do can cause grief for many girls. You might experience teasing from jealous boys who are months or even years behind you. Start by knowing that all kids hit their growth spurts eventually. It's really just a matter of time before everyone starts to balance out.

And remember, it's better to be a tall girl than a short guy! ☺

✿ Body Changes ....

✦ Aleah's Question: Growing Pains

Sometimes I wake up in the middle of the night and my legs are killing me! They throb and ache so bad that I can't go back to sleep. I'm too young for arthritis, right? That's like, what my grandma has, but that's what I think this feels like! What's wrong with my legs and how can I make it stop?

Isabel Says

Ouch! I went through this when I was 12 and I remember it killed. It feels like your bones are breaking apart or something!

Dr. Cohen says it's actually not the bones, but the muscles that ache. He said that 25 to 40 percent of all kids around this age get what are called "growing pains" and that for some reason it's worse at night. Yup, that's right: Growing pains are real, not just an expression!

Emily Says

Oh wonderful—something else to look forward to.

Aleah, Dr. Cohen also says to stretch before bed, massage your legs from the thighs down to your ankles, and use a heating pad.

Isabel Says

I know, isn't puberty great! ☺

🌼 Helpful Hint

During your growth spurt you may experience a painful leg cramp called a Charley Horse. These happen most often when you're stressed out or dehydrated. Tension builds in your muscles, and the wrong move can send your calf into a spasm.

The way to relieve a Charley Horse is to stretch your calves, raising your toes up toward your knee.

🌸 Girl to Girl

Even though most other girls won't admit it, we all feel really awkward and clumsy as we grow taller, get heavier, and our arms and legs get longer. It's hard to keep up with all of these changes and still be graceful!

★ Marie's Question: Weight Gain

I have gained a lot of weight in the last year—15 pounds to be exact! And it seems like it's all in my butt and thighs. I feel like a real fatty, and now my jeans fit all weird. I am really athletic, and I'm not lazy or anything, so why is this happening?!

Emily Says

Marie, I promise this weight gain has absolutely nothing to do with being lazy. I play soccer pretty much every day and this is happening to me right now, too.

Nature says that women need to be wider through the hip area to be able to have babies. But since that's like a million years off, just don't let weight gain get out of hand. Keep up with exercise and don't chow on cheeseburgers every day at lunch. You will even out before you know it.

Isabel Says

Weight gain is truly the most unfortunate part of puberty, in my humble opinion! I used to be rail-thin and now I have curves all over the place. It's weird watching your body completely morph before your eyes!

The one thing that keeps me calm is knowing it's totally normal for girls to collect pounds in their stomach, hips, butt, and thighs. And I prefer my womanly body to my little girl body anyway!

✿ Did You Know?

It's totally possible to grow as many as 4 inches in just 1 year! However, once you start having your period, you will only grow another 3 or 4 inches total.

The average American woman is 5 feet 4 inches tall, but keep in mind, height is a genetic trait, meaning that it is passed to you by your parents. If your parents are tall, you'll probably be too.

Fun Fact

Both boys and girls release hormones called androgens that cause their voice boxes to grow larger. This has little effect on girls' voices, but don't be surprised if your guy friends' voices start cracking all the time!

❀ Body Changes ....

Tips and Advice from Dr. Stuart Cohen

Some of the physical changes that accompany puberty are noticeably external, such as growing taller, wider, and gaining weight. But there are also many changes going on inside your body.

For example, the hormone estrogen causes your body to excrete a clear or white fluid from your vagina, called vaginal discharge. This helps your body flush out harmful bacteria. Another internal change is that your vaginal walls are becoming thicker. Your uterus and ovaries also get bigger.

You will also start ovulating regularly. Ovulation is the process in which your ovaries release the egg that gets flushed out with your period. Ovulation can feel like a slight pinching sensation for some girls, while others feel nothing. All these changes are preparing your body for the possibility of pregnancy when you are older.

Wrapping It Up

When it comes to puberty, girls are put through the wringer! Our bodies go through a complete metamorphosis. But you know, it can be really hard to deal with these changes if we are all silent about it. So, let's talk about what we're feeling with each other. It totally helps to say, "Why are my feet *so* much bigger than last year?" and hear other girls say that they are going through the same thing! ★

Health Issues

Happy and healthy!

P uberty can be so insane—that's why it is so important to take good care of ourselves. Many girls don't realize that their bad habits make these tough times even worse. Habits like eating junk food all the time, drinking soda instead of water, sacrificing our skin to the sun, and staying up all night or sleeping all day are just some ways in which we push our health aside.

❀ Health Issues

★ Isabel's Perspective

We do this because we're invincible, right? Wrong! We're soooo not immune to getting sick or developing diseases and other problems.

Take scoliosis for example—though we can't control whether we get it, we can make sure we show up on testing day and follow our doctor's instructions on how to manage it. I mean, how many of us skip scoliosis screening because we're too embarrassed to line up in our bathing suits? Once you find out that early detection is the only way to prevent scoliosis from getting worse, I bet you'll be the first in line at the next screening!

★ Emily's Perspective

Right sis! It's true that a lot of unhealthy conditions can be prevented or improved by simply making better decisions. And when it comes to food choices, teens definitely need some major help. It seems like all we eat sometimes is fatty fast-food and candy and snacks. Turns out, there are so many things to learn about the food we eat—and it's actually pretty interesting stuff.

Consider the fact that every decision we make now will affect our bodies 40 years from now. That makes it a little easier to remember to throw on a hat to avoid a sunburn that could cause skin cancer! The same is true for food—eating fast-food every day will make you fat, tired, and unhealthy. Not that you can't ever treat yourself to fries with ranch dressing, but learning to live and eat in a healthy way is just the smart thing to do.

Food Basics

"The only way to keep your health is to eat what you don't want, drink what you don't like, and do what you'd rather not."
~ Mark Twain

★ The Scoop

People who study food are called nutritionists, and the American government has a team of nutritionists and scientists who work for the United States Agriculture Department (USDA), as well as for the Food and Drug Administration (FDA). Their job is to study how our food is raised, processed, prepared, and consumed, and then make recommendations to the rest of us based on their research.

These recommendations include what foods people should eat based on their age, how many calories to consume, how much fat is OK, and other dietary stuff. It may sound complicated, but all of the information is broken down into easy-to-understand bites on Websites such as www.mypyramid. gov. Researching your diet will help you plan healthy menus that support your development through puberty.

❀ Helpful Hint

Beware of the serving size of your favorite foods. Most soda, juice, and iced tea are actually 2 servings contained in 1 bottle. This means the amount of calories you consume is doubled if you drink the whole thing!

The same holds true for your favorite snacks—the 99-cent bag of chips you devour at lunch may actually be a 2-serving snack loaded with calories and fat!

❀ Food Basics ....

⚙ Helpful Hint

Food is measured in calories, which represent the amount of energy food provides your body. They also tell you how much energy you need to burn in order to keep your weight the same, or to gain or lose weight. To support your body's energy needs during puberty you should consume 2,200 calories each day. If you eat more than that (and don't burn it off with exercise), you will gain weight.

◔ Did You Know?

To gain a pound you have to eat 3,500 calories and to lose a pound you have to burn 3,500 calories. Just think! If you ride your bike for an hour and you weigh 100 pounds, you will burn 294 calories!

★ May Ling's Question: Food Groups

My mom always says our meals come from 6 basic food groups. I'm confused because my school teaches us that there are only 4 groups. The thing is, the meals I eat at school are similar to what I eat at home. So, what's the diff? Who is right, and what's the point of food groups anyway?

Emily Says

You know what May Ling, they're both right. For about a million years everyone was taught to eat from the 4 basic food groups, which were meat, dairy, fruits and vegetables, and grains. After a while, they added 2 more groups to the list, because the government realized stuff was missing. So, they made fruits and veggies their own categories, added beans to the meat group, and gave fats and oils their own category. Now the basic 6 are grains, vegetables, fruit, dairy, meat and beans, and fats and oils. Our nutrition expert Lisa K says the food groups are to guide people so they can eat as healthy as possible.

Isabel Says

You know what else, girls? Fat is actually important for our bodies! She said about 30 percent of our total daily calories should come from healthy fats, because they're good for brain development and give us energy.

Food Basics ✿

★ Katie's Question: So Full

Sometimes when I eat I feel so full for a long time after. My mom said I probably digest slower than other people, but I was like, "What does that mean?"

Isabel Says

Hey Katie—I actually know this because my biology class just studied how digestion works! Digestion starts when you chew your food and saliva starts to break it down into smaller pieces. So, if you don't chew your food well enough your saliva doesn't have time to do its job and this can make your stomach feel all yucky.

Anyway, after you swallow, food goes into your stomach, where gastric acids break it down even more. If you overeat, this part will take longer and make that full feeling last longer. Then, food goes into your small intestine where most of the nutrients are absorbed into your bloodstream.

Whatever is leftover travels to your large intestine and finally out of your body when you go to the bathroom!

Emily Says

Katie, nutritionist Lisa K also says that it takes 20 minutes for your brain to register that you're full, so if you chew slowly, you can avoid overeating and feeling so full.

❀ Helpful Hint

Food allergies affect 12 million Americans, and 2.2 million of them are kids! The most common food allergies are milk, egg, peanut, shellfish, and soy allergies.

If you are allergic to a food it is really important to avoid it in all forms. This includes when it is an ingredient in something else, such as eggs in cake.

Did You Know?

People who don't eat meat are called vegetarians. Lacto-ovo vegetarians eat dairy products and eggs, while lacto vegetarians consume dairy but no eggs. And vegans do not ingest any animal products whatsoever—including honey.

✿ Food Basics ....

Tips and Advice from Nutritionist Lisa K

Deciding what to eat is further complicated by making the choice between commercially grown and organic foods.

Organic food is grown without pesticides or chemicals and has no genetically modified seeds. It is becoming more popular in America, although organic food is more expensive. If your family cannot afford to eat all-organic, choose from organic bell peppers, apples, strawberries, lettuce, peaches, potatoes, grapes, tomatoes, pears, carrots, cucumbers, spinach, green beans, squash, raspberries, meat, and dairy products. These types of foods, where you ingest the skin or entire food, subject you to the most chemicals when they're not organically grown.

If it is not possible to buy organic foods, there are still ways to lessen the amount of chemicals you take in. Just scrub fruits and vegetables under warm water with a scrubber brush or peel off the skin.

Wrapping It Up

If you read the nutritional labels on most pre-packaged meals—like frozen dinners and snack packs—you'll notice tons of unpronounceable words that sound more like a science experiment than food. When you see ingredients you can't even pronounce, beware! If you don't want to eat a bunch of chemicals, stick to fresh fruits, vegetables and meat. All those gross chemicals can make you look old, mess with your hormones, and even cause cancer! ★

Eating Healthy

"Your body is the direct result of what you eat,
as well as what you don't eat."
~ Gloria Swanson

★ The Scoop

For many teens, it's easier to eat the same things every day, or just grab fast-food and pre-packaged junk food in a hurry. However, eating on the go most definitely contributes to this nation's growing obesity epidemic, because so little thought is given to portion size and nutrition.

Think of food as fuel and your body as an expensive car. You wouldn't put cheap gas in a Mercedes, so don't fill your tank with junk food!

Plus, let's face it, kids can be pretty mean to overweight girls. Who wants to deal with being picked on and puberty all at the same time? But there are other important reasons for eating a low-fat, nutritious diet, such as reducing your risk of getting diabetes, heart disease, and painful joint conditions. Plus, eating complex carbohydrates, lean proteins, fresh fruits and vegetables, and minimal sugar benefits your entire body— from your brain to your skin to your hair and nails!

🌸 Helpful Hint

Experts recommend that girls consume at least 1,300 milligrams of calcium per day. This is because about 25 percent of your bone mass will form after puberty.

Building strong bones can help prevent osteoporosis (a disease that causes bones to become weak) later in life. Foods rich in calcium include dairy products, tofu, almonds, and beans.

✿ Eating Healthy ....

★ Haley's Question: Still Hungry!

I am trying to eat better, but when I have a salad for my meal it's not filling and I'm still hungry! The only time I actually feel full is when I eat stuff that's bad for me, like nachos and cheeseburgers. I want to eat healthier, but how can I when it doesn't ever fill me up?

Isabel Says

As a girl with an enormous appetite, I completely understand, Haley! Nutritionist Lisa K says to control hunger, it's actually better to eat small meals every 2 or 3 hours. This way, you end up eating 5 or 6 small meals a day, instead of 2 or 3 big ones.

I've been trying it, and it works! Eating smaller meals of protein and fiber more often keeps me from getting totally starving. That's good, because when you're starving, you tend to overeat. Plus, our physician Dr. Cohen says that eating more often keeps blood-sugar levels balanced and prevents afternoon crashes. So, keep eating that salad, plus smaller portions of more substantial foods during the day.

Emily Says

Hey girl, I like eating hearty snacks like fruit and veggies, hummus and crackers, or nuts. They all have fiber so you feel satisfied.

✿ Helpful Hint

The number one reason people say they choose fast-food and pre-packaged snacks over fresh meals is because "it's easier." So, remove the temptation and increase the nutritional value of your food choices by planning ahead! It is easy to eat better if you do a little prep work. For example, cut fresh veggies and store them in ready-to-go baggies—then toss them in your backpack for a mid-morning snack.

✿ Girl to Girl

Make your own trail mix by using almonds, walnuts, raisins, dried cranberries, dried pineapple, and other goodies. To maximize yumminess, use roasted, unsalted nuts. They're way better for you!

Eating Healthy

★ Emani's Question: Vegan

I'm vegan, which freaks my friends out, because they are worried that I am malnourished! They're always trying to get me to eat meat and other animal products, which bugs me. But they are really worried, so I thought I should at least make sure I am not going to be super-short or stop getting my period or something.

Emily Says

You have to give your friends a break, Emani, because they obviously just care about you. And some kids who go vegetarian or vegan don't understand that they have to eat more than just pasta and cookies. To be a healthy vegan, you really have to read labels carefully and make sure you get enough nutrients. Nutritionist Lisa K says as long as you do this, you'll be fine! Being a vegan who eats enough protein and calcium means you'll totally grow normally and, of course, still get your period.

Isabel Says

I actually decided to go vegetarian a year ago, Emani, so I know all about people freaking out. But I finally explained that eating tofu, beans, yogurt, veggies, nuts, and whole grains would probably make me the healthiest girl in my entire school! Now all my friends actually enjoy eating vegetarian meals with me!

✿ Helpful Hint

Make sure you have enough energy to survive the morning by eating a hearty, healthy breakfast. This keeps your mind alert and ready to learn. A great example of a power breakfast is scrambled eggs (protein), with chopped spinach (vegetable), and cheese (dairy), a slice of whole wheat toast (complex carbs) dipped in a little bit of olive oil (healthy fats), and a small apple (fruit).

Did You Know?

Our bodies need fat! Vitamins A, D, E, and K are "fat-soluble," so the body absorbs them only when they are paired with fat. Good fats—mono and poly-unsaturated—lower cholesterol. The fats you should limit are trans and saturated fats.

❀ Eating Healthy ....

Tips and Advice from Nutritionist Lisa K

Eating well does not have to be an all-or-nothing deal. Even making small changes that boost your calcium, iron, protein, and vitamin C intake is a great first step! And you can still enjoy soda and chips now and then—just don't make these your staple foods.

However, if you are used to eating foods high in fat, sodium, and sugar, it will take time for your palate to adjust to a healthy diet. This is not because foods that are good for you taste bad. It's because the average American diet unnecessarily overwhelms the taste buds! Thus, switching to diet soda or low-sodium baked chips may seem like a huge sacrifice in taste at first. But the good news is, your sense of taste adapts to whatever you choose to eat, whether it be salty chips or fresh produce.

Indeed, if you choose to eat better because you want to nourish your body, you will never feel deprived!

Wrapping It Up

Mostly, our parents do the grocery shopping, make meals, and pack lunches, so we might not think about what we eat. But, if you care about your health, you need to get involved and help your parents decide what food goes in the fridge or your lunch. Trust us, they will want your help! Plus, this way, you get to think about what you eat instead of randomly chowing down on whatever they give you. ★

Staying Hydrated

"Do not quench your inspiration and your imagination."
~ Vincent Van Gogh

★ The Scoop

Water does more than quench your thirst; it is the most important element in the human body! Get this—you could survive for an entire month or more without eating a single morsel of food, but you'd be toast in less than a week without water! That's because water is essential to all your bodily functions—including thinking, exercising, digesting food, and producing blood.

The human body is made up of approximately 70 percent water. Each time you pee or sweat, you lose some. So, to replenish your body, you must drink 6 to 8 glasses of water daily—more if you exercise or play sports.

Also, the health benefits of staying hydrated are awesome, including skin elasticity (i.e., no wrinkles!), more energy, and faster metabolism. Plus, water has zero calories and fat!

❀ Staying Hydrated ....

★ Abbey's Question: 8 Cups?

I know I'm supposed to drink, like, 8 cups of water every day, but I cannot get that much water down! It just makes me gag after awhile. What's the smallest amount of water I can get away with drinking?

Emily Says

Well, it depends on your activity level. I play sports, so I have to drink more water because I sweat so much. If you don't drink enough water to replace what you lost, your brain will get cloudy and your responses will be slow and clumsy. I used to not like water either, but then I learned that a lot of foods contain water! So you can actually "eat" some of your 8 cups of water by snacking on oranges, watermelon, celery, and other fruits and veggies that are mostly water.

⚓ Helpful Hint

Though bottled water is marketed as "pure," it is often no better than tap water. A recent study found that one-third of bottled water has bacteria or chemicals in it! Instead, drink filtered tap water from a reusable polyurethane bottle.

👉 Expert's Point of View

Tips and Advice from Nutritionist Lisa K

Putting water back into your body is critical to its functioning, and also increases your overall health. Staying hydrated during and after physical activity can help reduce joint and back pain. Hydration can work wonders for your mind and body!

Wrapping It Up

There are lots of ways to make water more appealing. We like to add lemon, lime, or orange slices to glasses of water. Other cool ways to jazz up water are to add cucumber slices, mint, or frozen watermelon cubes. Or, try a natural sparkling water, like Perrier. It's really refreshing! ★

Rest & Sleep

"Early to bed, early to rise,
makes a man healthy, wealthy and wise."
~ Benjamin Franklin

★ The Scoop

Getting enough sleep every night is a no-brainer and will help you perform well in sports and school. In fact, you won't be able to get A's in class if you don't get enough Z's at night! Research indicates that teenagers require 9 to 9½ hours of sleep every night in order to grow, stay healthy, and be alert the next day. Yet few teens actually get more than 7 hours of sleep! Not OK!

Each stage of sleep has its own benefits; therefore, you need enough time to move through each stage. Sleep activity ranges from light to deep sleep and dreaming. Many people get stuck in the first sleep stage when drifting off to sleep, which cuts into their actual sleep time. But you can change this if you eliminate habits that prohibit a good night's sleep and practice relaxation techniques.

So read, take a bath, or write in a journal before bed—all activities that help you wind down.

❀ Helpful Hint

Falling asleep within a reasonable amount of time can be as simple as using your bed only for sleep.

This means you should not do homework or watch TV while in bed. Limiting these activities to other parts of the house and making your room a haven of rest tells your brain, "I am tired. My bed is for sleep. Goodnight!" Train your brain so bed means time for sleep!

✿ Rest & Sleep ....

★ Ashanti's Question: Too Tired

I get really tired during the day, and sometimes I even fall asleep in class. It's embarrassing, and I've gotten in trouble a few times. But I can't help that I'm so tired! Even though I fall asleep easily at night, I wake up a few times thinking about stuff. What can I do to sleep through the night so I can stay awake during class?!

Isabel Says

It sounds kind of out there, but my mom taught me how to meditate and do deep-breathing exercises before bed, and it helps a lot. So, every night at 9 p.m., I stop what I'm doing, go to my room, and just sit with my eyes closed for about 15 minutes while I take super deep breaths. I get so relaxed, and it's much easier to sleep soundly.

✿ Helpful Hint

Avoid stimulants such as caffeine, chocolate, or sugar after 4 p.m. These will interfere with your ability to fall asleep at a reasonable hour, or may cause you to wake up within 30 minutes of falling asleep!

☞ Expert's Point of View

Tips and Advice from Dr. Stuart Cohen

Some teens don't sleep enough, but others actually sleep too much! Sleeping too much can cause you to feel groggy and lethargic throughout the day and may even lead to headaches and depression. Avoid sleeping more than 9½ hours a night.

Wrapping It Up

Some nights it's impossible to get enough sleep because you have to stay up late to finish a project or you're really nervous about a presentation. When this happens, you should take a nap after school to help pay off your "sleep debt." It's not ideal, but it takes the edge off in a pinch! ★

Safe Sun

"Live in the sunshine, swim the sea,
drink the wild air..."
~ Ralph Waldo Emerson

⚓ Helpful Hint

In addition to wearing sunscreen on a daily basis, you can use your clothing to defend your skin against harmful rays. The Skin Cancer Foundation recommends wearing dark, tightly woven fabrics for the most protection. These have the highest Ultraviolet Protection Factor (UPF) and can actually prevent up to 98 percent of UVB rays from reaching your skin!

★ The Scoop

Spending time in the sun usually means we're outside doing something fun! The warmth feels great on our skin, and we all like how we look with a little color. In fact, most people say that having a tan not only looks great but is a symbol of good health. But this is not true! Tans are not safe and damage skin, making a girl prone to wrinkles, sunspots, and even skin cancer.

Of course, it's not realistic to stay indoors or completely avoid any sun exposure. But you can protect your skin by getting in the habit of wearing a lotion with SPF 15 or more daily and wearing a hat and sunglasses when spending a long day in the sun.

Also, we know girls love tanning salons, but stay out of 'em! One-third of teen girls say they use tanning beds, however, the Skin Cancer Foundation says that exposure to tanning beds before age 35 increases the risk of getting melanoma skin cancer by 75 percent! So choose natural sun and protected skin or a sunless tanning lotion instead.

❀ Safe Sun ....

★ Kiki's Question: SPF?

I pretty much spend my entire summer outside. I know I should wear sunscreen, but I like a tan, and I never really burn, so do I have to wear it? Plus, I have no idea what SPF means. Can you explain?

Emily Says

SPF stands for Sun Protection Factor, and you definitely need it, even if you don't burn. You're still just as prone to skin cancer as a pale girl! An SPF 15 lotion gives you 15 times as long in the sun before you turn red—about 2 hours. Higher SPFs offer more protection, but you still have to reapply every 2 hours. Also, use waterproof sunscreen when you swim. I like to use the new spray-on sunscreens. They don't make your hands greasy and you won't miss a spot!

🌼 Helpful Hint

Think you don't need protection from the sun on cloudy days? This is a total myth! Even on the most overcast day, 40 percent of UV radiation still makes its way to earth, so cover up and apply sunscreen. No one wants to get fried!

☞ Expert's Point of View

Tips and Advice from Dr. Richard Fitzpatrick

Tanning beds expose you to harmful levels of UVA rays, which penetrate deeply into the skin, increasing the risk for melanoma—the deadliest form of skin cancer. Skip the tanning salon and use sunless tanners if you want a year-round golden glow.

Wrapping It Up

It's hard to care about stuff that won't really affect you until you're older. But skin cancer is totally gnarly and can be deadly. Our friend's mom has it and she always says she wished she had taken sun exposure seriously when she was our age. Plus, practicing safe sun prevents wrinkles! ★

Scoliosis

"Never grow a wishbone
where your backbone ought to be."
~ Clementine Paddleford

⚓ Helpful Hint

Weak muscles allow your spine to curve even more than it already wants to, so do exercises that strengthen your abdominal and back muscles. These will increase flexibility, improve your posture, and help prevent scoliosis from worsening. Examples of good exercises include arm, leg, and back extensions. These should be done on a stability ball for support and only with permission from your doctor.

★ The Scoop

You may wonder what the heck is going on when the school nurse lines you and your classmates up in your bathing suits. No, it's not a swimsuit contest! It is a way to determine whether you have a condition called scoliosis. No one knows why certain kids get it, but it is believed to be genetic.

Scoliosis is an abnormal side-to-side curving of the spine that affects approximately 2 percent of women and 0.5 percent of men. Instead of being straight, a spine with scoliosis is shaped like an S, or a question mark. If you are diagnosed with scoliosis, you may have uneven shoulders, one shoulder blade that sticks out more than the other, an uneven waist, one hip higher than the other, back pain, or a general feeling of fatigue.

Most kids who are diagnosed with mild cases of scoliosis do not require treatment, but some need to wear a brace to keep their spines in place.

❀ Scoliosis ....

★ Abbey's Question: Surgery?

I was diagnosed with scoliosis, and I guess it's pretty bad, because I have to have corrective surgery. I'm really scared and afraid it won't help. Why do I need surgery, and will it work?

Isabel Says

Tough break, Abbey, but Dr. Cohen says that if your spine is curved more than 40 or 50 degrees, you may need surgery. This is severe enough that your doctor wants to prevent it from getting worse. Spinal curves of 70 degrees or more can actually interfere with your breathing, so you definitely want to put the breaks on that now. The good news is that people usually see a dramatic improvement after surgery, so it'll be totally worth it!

🌼 Helpful Hint

Though there is no known cause of scoliosis, doctors have noted a genetic link within families. Early detection is essential to begin treatment, so let your school nurse know if you have a family history of spinal deformities.

👉 Expert's Point of View

Tips and Advice from Dr. Stuart Cohen

Spinal curves of 25 to 40 degrees may require wearing an orthopedic brace to prevent further curving. Braces are sometimes worn up to 23 hours a day, but should not prevent you from doing any of your normal activities.

Wrapping It Up

It must be really hard to be the only kid in your class with scoliosis. But you don't have to go through it alone! There are tons of peer groups you can join both in person or online for support. You may be the only one in your grade, but you are definitely not the only girl with this struggle. ★

Sports & Fitness

Go team!

Staying fit is important if you want to enjoy life to the fullest, from the time we're teenagers until we're 80 years old. Our doctor says that people who don't exercise can have weak bones, heart problems, and become overweight. Also, couch potatoes feel tired, lethargic, and bored. That's why we both exercise and are involved in sports and fun physical stuff whenever we can.

❀ Sports & Fitness ....

★ Emily's Perspective

I have been playing sports for as long as I can remember. No joke! There are baby pictures of me holding a soccer ball and smiling. I sometimes think I was born to play soccer. It gives me a total rush when I'm running down the field and know I'm going to score a goal.

But not everyone is born into sports. Many girls have to work at it. Interestingly, these girls are usually the ones who kick butt because they work so hard!

Being active affects how you spend your time, who your friends are, and often how strong and healthy you are. This is what I love most about any kind of physical activity—it requires discipline, commitment, and, best of all, helps you bond with friends.

★ Isabel's Perspective

Totally—when it's not fun, exercise can just feel like a chore. And no one likes to do chores! But if you choose activities that you like doing with people you like hanging out with, it gets to be that you actually look forward to working out or practicing.

For me, starting a fitness program on my own took discipline—it's not easy to go jogging before school or do sit-ups before bed. But doing these things pays off in so many ways! I look better, feel better, and I have become a person who follows through on goals. All these things boost my confidence. So, don't feel bad passing on a mall trip to hit the gym. Learning to make decisions that are best for YOU is the biggest part of getting fit.

Enjoying Sports

"I survived because I was tougher than anybody else."
~ Bette Davis

⚓ Helpful Hint

Whether you play basketball, ride a bike, or surf—always include time to warm up and cool down. Warming up before an activity literally warms up your muscles and gets them ready to play.

And equally important is cooling down because it brings your heart rate back down to normal levels. Plus, stretching afterward will prevent you from getting stiff and sore.

★ The Scoop

It's hard to imagine it today, but not so long ago, girls were totally discouraged, and some were even banned, from playing sports at school! When schools did have teams for girls, they usually had inferior equipment and uniforms. But that all changed in 1972 when Congresswoman Patsy T. Mink led an effort to make it illegal to exclude girls who want to play sports in any school that gets federal money.

This law, called Title IX, is actually part of the Civil Rights Act, because the government decided that girls have the right to play sports at school without harassment or discrimination. So, Title IX gives you the right to equally funded education and sports without fear of harassment or other abuse. You also have the right to appropriate uniforms and equipment. And finally, you have the right to kick some serious butt on the field or court!

❀ Enjoying Sports ....

❀ Helpful Hint

Gear up to play sports with the right equipment! This includes a sports bra to prevent your breasts from bouncing, which can be quite painful. Always wear a helmet when you ride a bicycle, and knee and elbow pads when you skateboard or rollerblade. And prevent hair from getting in your eyes by wearing a headband. Having the right stuff makes all the difference!

👁 Girl to Girl

Wearing spandex under your shorts prevents your thighs from rubbing together and causing a rash. Plus, if you are a bigger girl, spandex shorts will keep your stomach, hips, and thighs from jiggling around when you run.

★ Haley's Question: Shins!

I play basketball, and at practice we do running drills, laps and, of course, practice our jump shots. Lately, I've been getting these really bad pains from my knees down to my ankles. Sometimes, it hurts so bad I can barely walk! I stretch my calves and stuff before and after we play, so I have no idea why this is happening. Do you?

Emily Says

Ouch! Haley, it sounds like you've got shin splints! Even though it's really painful, it's totally treatable and not a big deal. Shin splints happen when the soft tissue attached to the bone is stretched too far.

Our fitness expert Lisa K says it's really common for basketball players to get them, usually from jumping and the start-and-stop motion of running drills. She said to wear good, new sneakers and to increase your flexibility by walking on your heels for a few minutes every day. These two things should help your shin splints go away. In the meantime, put ice on your shins as soon as you're done with practice.

Isabel Says

Also, Haley, know that there is no shame in sitting out when you are in pain or injured! In fact, you will be doing your team a favor by taking care of yourself.

Enjoying Sports ❀

★ Marie's Question: Bad Temper

Sometimes when I play softball I get so mad at the umpire! I feel like she's a complete idiot who has no idea what is going on and I tell her so! I talk smack to the other team when I'm feeling extra competitive. I don't see what the big deal is, but my coach said that if I don't stop I can't play anymore. What's the big deal in expressing frustration and the spirit of competition?

Isabel Says

Marie, a lot of girls are going to consider what you're doing poor sportsmanship! Of course you get frustrated and you won't agree with everything the ump says, but there is definitely a code of good sportsmanship that every athlete should follow. This is why you shake hands with the winning team when you lose and why coaches say "good job" even when you screw up.

Emily Says

For sure! I mean, the point of the game isn't only to win; it's also to be part of a community. And, to be honest, it sounds like you're bringing the whole team down with your negativity, sweetie.

Learn to show off your competitive spirit with your game-play, not your mouth. Your teammates, coaches, and other players will respect you way more.

❀ Helpful Hint

Stay hydrated when you play sports! When you sweat you lose valuable water through your skin. On hot days you should drink 1½ to 2½ additional cups of water. And if you plan to run a long race or go for a tough hike, carry a sports drink that contains sodium, since you also lose this essential mineral when you sweat.

Fun Fact

In 1973, female tennis star Billie Jean King beat Bobby Riggs in a televised tennis match called The Battle of the Sexes. Riggs had bragged that he could beat any female player and came out of retirement to play King. Unfortunately for Riggs, it didn't quite go his way!

❁ Enjoying Sports ················

Tips and Advice from Fitness Expert Lisa K

If you play sports, you are in good company! More girls are playing sports every year. In fact, recently, a record-setting 6,903,552 girls participated in team athletics at their high schools. Though basketball is most popular, soccer is catching up.

This is good news, because as more girls play sports, it normalizes the athletic body type, which means more strong girls who are in-shape and confident! Additionally, if more girls play sports, their programs will receive more funding, which helps make girls sports more than just a sidenote to boy's teams.

Luckily, studies show that girls who play sports are less prone to bouts of depression, are more satisfied with their bodies, have higher self-esteem, and hold a more positive outlook in general. So, stay on the team—it's good for you, and you are a part of a national trend!

Wrapping It Up

Because Emily loves soccer, she's had kids tease her about being a tomboy. But whatever—we know they're just not sure what to do with a girl who is both pretty and likes playing sports! Besides, playing sports is more than just being athletic. It's about being a part of a team effort, making friends, going on fun trips, and working on goals. It's cool to be the kind of girl who does all that! ⭐

Staying Fit

"I love the feeling of freedom in running, the fresh air, the feeling that the only person I'm competing with is me."
~ Wilma Rudolph

❀ Helpful Hint

Set specific and realistic goals for your exercise program. Then, break these goals down into steps. When you accomplish each step, check it off. Post these accomplishments where you will see them and feel proud! Whatever your goal is, build in enough time to work up to it so you don't get discouraged.Sticking to the plan will allow you to meet your goals in a realistic way while minimizing frustration.

★ The Scoop

For some, just thinking about exercising makes them tired. However, exercise actually releases chemicals called *endorphins* that elevate your mood and are a natural pain reliever.

For instance, have you ever heard the term, "runner's high"? The fact is, you totally don't have to be a star athlete to benefit from endorphins. Regular exercise also provides the same benefits. Within 20 to 30 minutes of doing physical activity, you can expect to feel an improvement in your mood and energy level. If this is true of the first 20 to 30 minutes, just imagine how you'll feel after participating in a long-term fitness program!

Exercise not only makes you feel amazing, but it can be really fun, too. You don't have to join a gym or go running—you can stay fit by dancing, skating, bowling, bike riding, and any other activity that is fun and gets you going!

❀ Staying Fit ·······················

⚙ Helpful Hint

Weight training gives you more muscle mass and makes your muscles stronger. But don't worry, you won't start looking like a bodybuilder! Lifting weights a few times a week will give your arms and legs a subtle shape and definition, which looks really good—and really feminine. Plus, muscle mass actually burns fat. Even if you're just sitting there watching TV, your muscles are burning up calories. Total bonus!

👁 Girl to Girl

Hate all the eyes on you at the gym? Work out at home to a DVD! They range from aerobics to kickboxing to Tai Chi, and are great for every fitness level!

★ Kiki's Question: Motivation

It seems like it's impossible for me to get motivated to exercise consistently. I go to the gym for a few weeks, but then I just get lazy and stop. I get mad at myself and think I should start up again, but I'm like, "What's the point?" since I'll just quit again. Then I feel like I wasted all kinds of time. Is there any way to stay motivated? I hate having to start from scratch every time.

Emily Says

OK Kiki, beating yourself up is not going to get you anywhere! Being so negative will actually discourage you from exercising.

When I need to motivate, I remind myself why I want to work out. Is a dance coming up? Do I have to wear a bathing suit soon? Have I been feeling really tired? Knowing why you want to exercise is the driving force that keeps you jumping rope, even though you'd rather be taking a nap.

Isabel Says

That's great advice, sis! Every girl's motivators are different, Kiki. And there are definitely days when I sleep in and skip going to the gym. When that happens, I just remind myself to get back on track the next day. A great tip that works for me is to keep a workout calendar. I check off every day I exercise and write what I did. It makes me happy to see all the X's!

★ Ashanti's Question: Yoga

What's the deal with yoga? It's gotten really trendy at my school, but I think it looks kind of boring. Is it just meditation or what? Can yoga really get me in good shape?

Isabel Says

You're right, Ashanti—yoga has gotten really popular with celebrities like Jennifer Aniston and Gwyneth Paltrow, and that's because it is an amazing workout with tons of benefits! Doing yoga regularly gives you long, lean muscles; increases flexibility; reduces stress; and improves your posture. No more slouching!

In a yoga session, you will hold various postures—called *asanas*—while focusing on breathing, balance, alignment, and different muscle groups. The result is a really toned, defined body. You should definitely try it!

Emily Says

Hey Ashanti, I used to think yoga looked lame, too. Lots of sitting around, right? But then my soccer coach suggested that my team take a yoga class, because he said it would help us control our bodies and learn focus and balance. And it was really cool! It was a great workout, and I felt a lot more calm and centered afterward.

I guess there's a reason yoga has been around for more than 3,000 years!

❀ Helpful Hint

Don't get discouraged—most workouts can be modified to accommodate beginners, like or walking instead of running at first. And besides, you should always begin an exercise program with the idea that you will keep improving upon your skills. That way, you will always be challenged to continue to work on your goals as they grow with your level of fitness.

🌸 Did You Know?

Your heart is a muscle like any other and will get weaker if it is neglected. Cardiovascular exercise, like climbing stairs or jogging, pumps blood more quickly, which is basically strength-training for your heart. This can even extend your life!

❁ Staying Fit ....

Tips and Advice from Fitness Expert Lisa K

Always put safety first when it comes to exercising. This includes wearing the right shoes, caring for blisters, sitting out when you are injured, and having someone spot you when lifting weights. Exercising with caution also includes warming up, cooling down, and stretching before and after your workout.

However, even if you take precautions, it is still possible to get injured during athletic activity. If you ever feel a pop in one of your joints or your lower back hurts, stop what you are doing, tell a parent or your coach, and put ice on the affected area. Taking immediate action can facilitate healing and prevent a trip to the emergency room.

Though it is frustrating, some injuries require you to take a week or more off to heal. This is a must! Exercising when injured will only cause further damage, which is counterproductive to your health goals.

Wrapping It Up

Boredom can stop you from exercising, so we like to do stuff that doesn't feel like exercise and involves our friends. On the weekends, we all ride our bikes together and go bowling and hiking a lot. Also, sometimes we meet and walk around the track before school to catch up on important gossip! It's exercise, but it's so fun because we're together. Rally a few of your girlfriends and make a fun fitness plan. ★

Emotional Issues

Hugs make everything better!

S ome of the most difficult changes we have to deal with during
puberty are the emotional ones. Emotional issues can be hard
to manage, because we can't always explain them, we just feel
them. The thoughts and feelings that sneak up on girls during puberty
can make us feel very alone, confused, and out of control.

✿ Emotional Issues ....

★ Emily's Perspective

For a while there, I would just burst into tears for no reason. Mood swings are really stressful because you can't explain what's wrong. I think my parents were even stressed out! But then therapist Catherine Butler told me that I am actually NOT in control of some of these emotions. It was a relief to hear that!

The trick is to learn to go with the flow and not bury these feelings in an attempt to pretend they don't exist. You have to find a healthy way to cope with emotional stress—like exercise, listening to music, or art, for example—to keep anxiety in check.

★ Isabel's Perspective

So true Emily. Stress is so crazy—it can actually make you sick!

I think another important part of working through this stuff means talking about emotions, stressors, and fears, either with a parent, friends, or even just writing in a journal.

Every girl feels sad, lonely, and super-stressed from time to time. I definitely have "fat days," and days when I feel like no one understands me. It can really help to find out that other girls are in the same boat.

Just remember, you don't have to go through this alone, and you don't have to feel weird or scared about how you're feeling. Depression, anxiety, mood disorders, and eating disorders are very real and very serious. Find a shoulder to lean on or a trusted adult to talk to. And most important— know that many of the emotions that come with crazy puberty hormones will soon pass!

Handling Stress

*"When you get to the end of your rope—
tie a knot and hang on."
~ Eleanor Roosevelt*

★ The Scoop

If not dealt with, stress can cause sleepless nights, physical pain, and illness. And Americans are some of the most stressed out people on the entire planet!

For one, we're always plugged into our high-tech gadgets. I bet a lot of you girls even sleep with your cell phones! This high-tech world, plus our busy schedules packed with activities, can really stress us out, threatening both our health and our sanity. Add that to all the physical and emotional upheaval that puberty brings, and you've got a lot of teenagers who are chronically stressed.

You don't want to be one of them, though—stressed out people are often tired and depressed on a daily basis. One tip is to find time for yourself and tune out the world (aka, turn off your cell phone!). If you learn to practice relaxation and stress-management, you will enjoy more peace, happiness, and energy.

❀ Helpful Hint

Studies show that laughter reduces stress, lowers blood pressure, elevates mood, boosts the immune system, improves brain functioning, increases oxygen in the blood, fosters connections with others, and makes you feel good all over.

So, watch a funny movie, read a daily joke, or laugh with your friends every day to reduce stress and promote relaxation.

❀ Handling Stress....................

★ Marie's Question: So Stressed!

By the time I get home from school I am so fried I feel like I could scream! All we do is take notes, take tests, write papers, and make presentations. I'm mentally exhausted! Obviously, I can't stop going to school, so how can I relieve the stress I feel?

Emily Says

Take some time after school to chill out. I flip through a magazine or play with my dog—things that don't require tons of brain-power but are fun and relaxing. Just avoid becoming a couch potato the second you're home. Catherine Butler says that fresh air can stimulate and decompress you at the same time, so maybe take a walk outside. It's so nice after being cooped up in class all day!

❀ Helpful Hint

Reduce stress with deep breathing. Take deep breaths that start low in your belly. Exhale until every drop of air has left your lungs. This type of breathing gets more oxygen to your brain and releases endorphins, which make you feel good all over.

👉 Expert's Point of View

Tips and Advice from Therapist Catherine Butler

Take a few quiet minutes to yourself every day to de-stress and reset. We are surrounded by the constant noise of the television, computer, or stereo. So, go to your room, close the door, and sit quietly for awhile without any distractions.

Wrapping It Up

Ever hear of Feng Shui? It involves clearing away your clutter so healthy energy can flow around you. Basically, you'll be less stressed if your room is clean! We recently organized our rooms and gave away old clothes. Now everything has a place and we don't get stressed out by a big mess. Try it! ★

Emotions

"I'm selfish, impatient, and a little insecure. I make mistakes, I am out of control, and at times hard to handle. But if you can't handle me at my worst, then you don't deserve me at my best."
~ Marilyn Monroe

★ The Scoop

Irritability, temper tantrums, and unexplained tears might be part of your daily existence these days. That's because puberty doesn't only change your body—it also wreaks havoc on emotions! Part of this is that most girls become extremely self-conscious about their bodies. You might be covering up in an oversized sweatshirt to hide big boobs. Or maybe you've started changing for gym in the bathroom stall because you don't have any boobs yet. The urge to compare yourself to other girls can make this time really tough.

Know that being comfortable with the new you is complicated and will take some time. In the meantime, if you start to feel upset or frustrated, find a quiet place where you can chill out until the emotional moment passes. And if you need to cry for a second, that's OK—it's actually a healthy release. Just don't lose sight of the fact that every girl your age is feeling out of place right now, too!

🌸 Helpful Hint

Even though it is hard to talk about feeling angry or sad, find a loving adult or friend and explain what is bothering you. Research shows that keeping negative feelings inside too long causes insomnia, anxiety, loss of or increase in appetite, depression, muscle tension, diarrhea, and stomach ulcers. Plus, it just feels good to get bad feelings off your chest, right?

❁ Emotions ....

❁ Helpful Hint

Surging hormones and confusion about who you are may cause you to feel angry a lot of the time. Instead of carrying it around inside or acting out in mean ways, take up martial arts or kickboxing. Contact sports are great exercise and allow you to safely express aggression without hurting anyone. Plus, they teach valuable lessons in respect and discipline that benefit your entire life.

Girl to Girl

Something about puberty turns nice girls into jealous trolls! Of course, a little jealousy is normal and understandable. Just keep it in check, because if you let it get out of hand you will lose friends and feel pretty awful about yourself.

★ May Ling's Question: Daddy's Girl

I've always been a daddy's girl. I used to talk to my dad about everything and loved hanging out with him, but now it seems totally weird. Plus, I hate it when he tries to ask me about anything having to do with body changes. I know he cares, but I felt like I was going to die when he asked if I needed pads from the grocery store! How can I explain all of this to him without hurting his feelings?

Isabel Says

This is such a sad fact of puberty for dads, I think. I really do feel bad for them, but you have to trust that he'll understand if you explain it to him. You don't have to be mean—just tell him that you need space and you're too embarrassed to talk about certain stuff with him. He'll get what you mean.

Emily Says

But you should definitely keep spending time with him May Ling! I know our dad was really hurt when Isabel and I stopped wanting to hang out with him on the weekends. I mean, we have parties and friends' houses to go to. But now we find stuff we all like to do together, like seeing a movie or going out for ice cream. That way, we get to be together, but we don't have to talk about girl stuff! Phew.

★ Emani's Question: Nerves

I feel like a crazy person, because whenever I have to talk in front of people I get super-nervous, turn beet-red, start sweating like a maniac, and feel like I'm going to have a heart attack. I hate it, and I have a ton of presentations to do in school! What the heck is going on with me?

Emily Says

Whoa! Take a deep breath, girlie. It's really common to melt down when you have to talk in front of people—especially during puberty when you're so self-conscious.

In fact, I read somewhere that fear of public speaking beats out fear of death for most people! Therapist Catherine Butler says to make sure you practice in the mirror several times before the big day. Then, when you get up there, take a bunch of deep breaths and be confident that you know your presentation. Focus on one object, and pretend you're talking to an empty room. Some people say to picture your audience in their underwear, but that would just make me laugh!

Isabel Says

Ew, I don't want to picture any of my classmates in their underwear! I say, forget you're making a school presentation. Just pretend you're talking to a bunch of friends about whatever. Stay focused, but be casual.

❁ Helpful Hint

Managing mood swings can feel like a full-time job. But, getting at least 8 hours of sleep every night, avoiding sugar and caffeine, exercising, and eating a healthy diet can help keep you calm. These things stabilize your blood-sugar levels, which, when they are out of whack, can influence the intensity of mood swings. Mood swings are normal during puberty; however, if you feel sad for more than 2 weeks, tell a parent so you can get professional help.

🏈 Did You Know?

Scientists have actually discovered chemicals in the brain that cause increased levels of anxiety in teenagers. So, you're totally not crazy!

❁ Emotions ....

Tips and Advice from Therapist Catherine Butler

One of the most difficult aspects of managing the emotions that accompany puberty is the feeling that life will always be hard. But it's not true—and as bad as you ever feel, it is important to have perspective. Having perspective means that you understand that your current state is not permanent.

For example, maybe you are upset because you are being teased for having small breasts. See the situartion in a positive light. Remind yourself that you are still growing and developing, and you can make up for your size with how you dress and the bra you wear. This helps you see that nothing is hopeless.

Indeed, gaining perspective is a crucial tool to have in order to navigate the murky waters of puberty. Without perspective, life feels complicated, lonely, and scary. So, practice having perspective the next time you hear yourself say "never" or "always." Thinking this way is an exaggeration of the facts. And puberty is hard enough without exaggeration!

Wrapping It Up

Everything is worse if you feel like you're going through it alone. You might feel like the only person who has ever been embarrassed about getting her period or depressed about her boob size. But those feelings can be enough to make a connection with another person. We've become closer as sisters because of these changes. Making connections with people can help you laugh about things, instead of feeling bummed out! ★

Mood Swings

"Well-behaved women rarely make history."
~ Laurel Thatcher Ulrich

⚓ Girl to Girl

Sleep is important to staying rational. When you're tired and worn out, you will find your mood swings are way worse. You might freak out if a teacher corrects you or if your best friend forgets to call you back.

So make sure you are getting the recommended 9 hours of sleep a night. A good night's sleep will keep you calm and level-headed.

★ The Scoop

You're up, you're down, you're a normal teenager! Mood swings are par for the course during puberty. They can be extremely frustrating for you, and for those around you. But it's not you, exactly—it's the hormones your body releases during puberty. Of course, the day-to-day stress of school, peer pressure, and changing roles within your family definitely cause mood swings to be exaggerated. However, though you may not have control over your feelings, you do have control over how you deal with them.

Learning how to channel the flood of emotions that hit you at any given moment may take some practice, but it is well worth the effort. After all, you don't want to become the hormonal monster depicted in lame teen comedies, do you? Of course not! So, you will need to develop coping skills for when you are sent reeling into the emotional extremes of puberty.

❀ Mood Swings.........................

★ Aleah's Question: Rollercoaster Emotions

One minute I'm laughing, the next I'm crying, and then an hour later I'm ready to scream and tear my hair out. These moods swings make me crazy and are even driving my best friend away! How can I make this stop?!

Emily Says

Aleah, our bodies are surging with hormones right now. So, sometimes you're feeling really good and then suddenly you're bawling in the corner. First, make sure your friend knows it's not her fault if you get upset. Be willing to apologize to her when things go wrong. It's just a normal part of puberty that she'll go through soon too. And, if you can get to a private place to cry your heart out, you'll release all those pent-up feelings.

✿ Helpful Hint

Prevent outbursts by spending some time alone. This requires you to say no to social plans when you are not feeling your best. After all, taking care of your needs is the best way to ward off major mood swings.

👉 Expert's Point of View

Tips and Advice from Therapist Catherine Butler

Your parents or other caring adults, like teachers and coaches, can help you through this difficult time if you let them. Talk about feelings and triggers. Ask for space when you need it and let them know you appreciate their patience with your fluctuating moods.

Wrapping It Up

Mood swings are made much worse by pretending you and others don't have them. Seriously, why do we treat the girl who flips out after dropping her lunch like she is a freak? We're all in the same situation, so let's start acting like it by first admitting we all have mood swings. ★

Depression

*"The soul would have no rainbow
had the eyes no tears."*
~ John Vance Cheney

⚓ Helpful Hint

Do you run from one activity to the other after school, and then rush home, only to stay up late doing homework? If so, give yourself a break! "Overachievers" can easily become overwhelmed with feelings of failure and the pressure to be perfect at everything they do—which can lead to depression. Take just one activity off your plate and you will feel a great sense of relief—and keep your sanity!

★ The Scoop

Reports of depression and anxiety among teenagers are on the rise. Approximately 1 in 3 teenagers suffer from clinical depression, and among these teens, suicide rates have tripled.

You probably feel so much pressure to succeed in school, get into a good college, excel at sports, be popular, lose weight, and much more. Feeling overwhelmed leads to chronic stress and exhaustion, and this results in depression and anxiety. If left untreated, depression and anxiety cause loss of appetite, falling grades, isolation, and thoughts of suicide. However, with proper treatment, depression can be managed, and you will soon feel better and less alone.

Even though it seems like no one could possibly understand what you are going through, please talk about your feelings, no matter how scary they seem. And if you need to turn to a pro, there are many wonderful counselors out there who are just waiting to offer their help.

❁ Depression ....

★ Abbey's Question: The Blues

How do I know whether I am depressed or just feeling down in the dumps?

Isabel Says

I was really down for a while and Catherine Butler gave me a handout that helped me sort out whether I was depressed or just temporarily sad. Here are some questions you should ask yourself to tell the difference: Have you been sad every day for 2 weeks or longer? Do you feel empty inside and like there is no point to anything? Have you lost or gained weight? Do you have trouble sleeping, or sleep too much? Do you feel guilty for things that aren't your fault? Is it hard to concentrate or make decisions? Do you ever think about killing yourself? If you answered "yes" to 5 or more, you may be depressed and in need of treatment.

👉 Expert's Point of View

Tips and Advice from Therapist Catherine Butler

Use of antidepressants to treat teenagers is controversial, but sometimes necessary. If your depression is severe, your family and doctor should discuss all treatment options, including the possibility of medication and the help of a great counselor.

Wrapping It Up

Anything can trigger depression, like not making the cheerleading team or failing a test. I know it doesn't seem like it when you're sad, but things will get better. Depression isn't your fault, and, thankfully, the people who love you are here to help. Remember, you will feel better in time. ★

Eating Disorders

"Go within every day and find the inner strength so that the world will not blow your candle out."
~ Katherine Dunham

★ The Scoop

We live in a world where body image is constantly being distorted. Models and celebrities create our body-image standards, and yet even they are always being accused of being fat!

With all this pressure, we have to pay close attention to our thoughts and feelings about beauty and health so that we are able to catch ourselves (and our friends) when the desire to be thin turns into a dangerous obsession.

Eating disorders develop over time, and always have warning signs, such as becoming obsessed with weight, calories, food, dieting, appearance, and never being happy. Learn to recognize these.

Girls as young as 6 and women as old as 76 have reported suffering from eating disorders. If you have one, you are not alone, but you do need help.

🌼 Helpful Hint

Eating disorders often develop in girls who feel like they have no control over their lives. Their parents tell them what activities to participate in or what clothes to wear. This can be incredibly frustrating, and so girls turn toward what they can control—food. If you feel like your life is out of control, talk to your parents about giving you more control over the decisions that directly affect you.

✿ Eating Disorders ·················

★ Emani's Question: Making Myself Sick

I feels like I have been trying to lose weight for like, a hundred years, but nothing works. I am still fat. I can't stand to gain one more pound, so I eat my lunch in the bathroom and then immediately throw it up. I feel like I will stop doing this once I get a handle on my weight, but I wonder if it's a problem?

Isabel Says

We know you must be worried, Emani, so the best thing to do is be honest with your doctor so you can get this figured out.

Therapist Catherine Butler says bulimia is when a person eats a lot and then throws up because they feel bad about eating so much. Teens who throw up so often will ruin their teeth, esophagus, and throat. And, if left untreated, bulimia can be fatal. So, please Emani, talk to a parent or doctor, or call the Eating Disorders Awareness and Prevention hotline at 1-800-931-2237.

Emily Says

It makes me sad, Emani, that wanting to be thin makes you feel like you don't deserve to eat lunch with the rest of the kids. Isabel is so right—you definitely need to address this problem. Bulimia is a serious sickness that keeps people from ever being happy with their weight and shape!

Eating Disorders ✿

★ Aleah's Question: Obsessed

My friend is totally obsessed with her appearance. She's always finding mirrors and windows and criticizing how she looks. She talks a lot about wanting plastic surgery to fix her nose or liposuction to get rid of her fat. Sometimes she even says that she'd rather be dead than look the way she does. She's so pretty—I don't know if she really means that stuff. Should I be worried about her?

Emily Says

Aleah, our expert Catherine Butler says lots of girls stress out about parts of their bodies that they don't like, but if it's really severe, it might be an issue called body dysmorphic disorder (BDD). BDD affects 2 percent of Americans—70 percent of whom are under age 18. BDD makes people obsessed with a minor aspect of their appearance—and sometimes the flaw is totally imagined! Without treatment, people with BDD may take drastic measures to alter their appearance, so your friend should talk to a doctor, who can steer her in the right direction.

Isabel Says

Aleah, every girl has parts of her body she doesn't love, but there is a real difference between that and BDD, which can cause depression and social anxiety. Urge your friend to visit a trained professional!

❀ Helpful Hint

One out of every 100 girls between the ages of 10 and 20 suffers from anorexia. This is a serious condition in which a person denies herself so much food that her body is literally starving. When left untreated, this condition results in death. The good news is that 80 percent of people who seek treatment are successful and recover. If you or someone you know is anorexic, seek help.

🦋 Did You Know?

An eating disorder affects more than just the person who has it. Families are often torn apart by guilt, fear, and sorrow because of these diseases. Friends of the person become confused and scared, and some even copy the behavior.

❀ Eating Disorders ....

Tips and Advice from Therapist Catherine Butler

Recovery is essential to the health of the person affected by an eating disorder. In fact, people who do not get treatment can die from their condition. Eating disorders are a painful existence for the sufferer and agonizing for friends and family to watch. However, once treatment has begun, there is light at the end of the tunnel.

Treatment for an eating disorder may include hospitalization, different forms of therapy, and medication. The goal is to rid the person of her fear or addiction to food, and to help her value her life and to eat—and keep down—a varied diet. This can take many years, and there are often setbacks and relapses.

Most important to know is that people who suffer from eating disorders have a sickness. They are not just craving attention or seeking to drop a couple of pounds. They have a serious illness that requires treatment.

Wrapping It Up

Being friends with someone who has an eating disorder is difficult. Everything revolves around her secrets, what she eats or doesn't eat, if she's sad, or if she's proud of not eating—it's really intense! That's why if you suspect your friend has an eating disorder you have to tell someone—your mom, her mom, or the school nurse. We definitely aren't equipped to handle something this big on our own. ★

Friends & Self-Esteem

Best Friends Forever!

Confidence is probably the most important part of navigating the teenage years, because now, more than ever, you will be faced with adult decisions. This can be anything from pressure to drink, to cheating in school, to participating in nasty gossip about other kids. Girls with low self-esteem can easily fall victim to peer pressure, stress, and depression.

❀ Friends & Self-Esteem..........

★ Emily's Perspective

It's so true that when we feel bad about ourselves, it can affect our whole lives. A lot of girls with low self-esteem make some seriously bad decisions, like getting drunk or doing drugs or having sex. They might feel cool for a second, until they get in trouble, start getting bad grades, or lose tons of friends. And that just makes depression and anxiety worse. It's like, a nasty cycle.

I think self-esteem is also about letting people know what you stand for. I admire girls who are strong and confident—like Isabel. I've learned a lot about self-esteem from my sister. For example, she makes it a point not to talk about other girls, even when everyone else is joining in on the gossip. That's one thing that it's OK to turn up your nose at!

★ Isabel's Perspective

Thanks Em, but I definitely still screw up. Recently, I did something pretty stupid—trying a cigarette—and, of course, I got caught. My dad was really disappointed, but he also said something interesting—if I don't love and respect myself, no one else will either, and I won't have the guts to stick up for myself and do what's right. That made a lot of sense to me. Puberty and emotional changes are so stressful, but you can't lose sight of who you are! Surround yourself with strong girlfriends and talk to someone you trust when you feel pressured. And remember, the kids who think smoking or getting drunk are cool only feel sad and empty later. Life is tough enough without that stuff bringing you down.

We have to learn to accept ourselves and have real self-confidence so we'll be prepared to deal with pressure and the urge to act rebellious. And with healthy friendships and confidence, you will be a much better student, daughter, sister, and friend!

Confidence

"Throw your dreams into space like a kite, and you do not know what it will bring back, a new life, a new friend, a new love, a new country."

~ Anais Nin

✱ Helpful Hint

Increase your opinion of yourself by loving the way you look. Look in the mirror and find something you like. Say, "I have cool hair," or "I like my lips." Eventually, you will learn to love the whole image.

It may take a few times to get used to doing this exercise without feeling corny, but regular practice will make a huge difference in the way you view yourself.

★ The Scoop

Taking control and believing that you can create the best possible life for yourself is the way to have true confidence. Think about it and it will make sense: Live your life to its fullest potential by taking risks, trusting your judgment, and believing you deserve to be valued.

For many girls, low self-esteem is the result of focusing on aspects of your life you just can't change, like ethnicity, height, bone structure, or economic status. By obsessing about these things, you will start to think you are not as good as someone else.

But confidence isn't about being the hottest girl in your class or the best athlete on your team. Find what you love about yourself and build confidence from there. Also, emulate a confident woman you know. She probably walks into a room with her shoulders back and a smile on her face, no matter what she's wearing. If you act confident, your emotions will soon follow your actions!

✿ Confidence..................................

★ Kiki's Question: Disappointed

Sometimes I look around and think, "This is my life?!" I thought I'd be a straight-A student and be awesome at the guitar by 8th grade, but instead, I'm an average student and I can't play a single chord! I look at these other girls who are popular and smart, and I feel like I'm just a boring girl with nothing going for me. What can I do?

Emily Says

Oh Kiki, you are WAY too young to have an "it's over" attitude! Instead of focusing on what you aren't, focus on what you are. I mean, just because you're not where you thought you'd be doesn't mean you're stuck. Make changes! Get guitar lessons, study more, and remember that it is NEVER too late to make your life whatever you want it to be, whether you are 13 or 30.

✿ Helpful Hint

Keep a running list of things you do that make you proud. And do not downplay that you received an A in art class or learned how to make lasagna—put it on the list! Hang your list where you will see it to remind yourself of all you have accomplished.

👉 Expert's Point of View

Tips and Advice from Therapist Catherine Butler

Increase self-esteem by being kinder to yourself. Replace "I can't spell; I'm so dumb" with positive self-talk, such as, "I'm good at math." Unchecked self-criticism does not help you. In fact, it prevents you from experiencing the joy self-confidence brings.

Wrapping It Up

Sometimes, when you aren't confident, it's because you're afraid. But, the only one stopping you is YOU. Who cares what other people think? Who cares if you aren't a pro right away? Not trying something new—like rock climbing or salsa dancing—because you're scared is lame! ★

Social Situations

"Don't compromise yourself. You're all you've got."
~ Janis Joplin

⚓ Helpful Hint

Preparing for your first dance can be fun or a total nightmare. First, you need a date; second, a dress; third, shoes; and finally, permission to stay out late!

To reduce anxiety over having a date, consider asking the boy you like—no sense waiting around! If you don't have a date, don't be discouraged! Go with a group of friends instead. It might be more fun anyway!

★ The Scoop

The most exciting and terrifying moments we face as teenagers are the social ones—dances, presentations, recitals, first dates, first kisses, and first boyfriends! They are exciting, because there is nothing like your first kiss, and you will always remember the first boy you ever loved. Still, some of these moments are terrifying, because they push you way outside your comfort zone.

But whether you are a social butterfly or more of a wallflower you will have to deal with peer pressure at some point, so be ready to stand strong! Peer pressure creates the most difficult social situations—and just when you are trying to figure out where you fit in this world!

Just remember that the decisions you make that dictate whether you are "in" or "out" stick with you until you leave school. So, make intelligent choices that follow your values and instincts.

✿ Social Situations...................

★ Aleah's Question: Smoking

A group of girls just recently asked me to come smoke behind school with them during lunch. I don't want to smoke cigarettes, but I also don't want them to think I'm a nerd or a loser. How can I avoid smoking but still make these girls think I'm cool?

Isabel Says

That's really weird, Aleah, because at my school, it's the kids who smoke who are considered losers. But anyway, if you want to hang out with these girls, you are going to have to be strong enough to say no and be willing to walk away with your head held high, even if they call you names for not smoking. And if they do that then you know, deep down, that they aren't going to make good friends anyway.

✿ Helpful Hint

If a boy wants to get physical before you are ready, you shouldn't be scared to say no way. And don't worry too much about it—our expert Catherine Butler says boys are often just testing boundaries and are actually relieved when a girl says no!

👉 Expert's Point of View

Tips and Advice from Therapist Catherine Butler

Sometimes the most effective way to handle peer pressure is to NOT be in the position to have to say no at all! In other words, be a leader. Be a girl that others follow. And if you stand by your decisions, others will respect your judgment.

Wrapping It Up

It is not worth doing something just to fit in. There are always consequences that outweigh the benefits, such as guilt, remorse, regret, shame, embarrassment, and even punishment. And if you do get caught, the people you were trying to impress will totally not rescue you! ★

Friendships

"Friendship is a single soul dwelling in two bodies."
~ Aristotle

★ The Scoop

Our friendships are pretty much the most important things in our lives, right? It is our friends who get us through sad days, broken hearts, and family problems. A lot of times, we feel like our friends know us better than our own parents!

Creating strong, long-lasting friendships is so important to our health and happiness. People who have a close-knit group of friends have less stress and recover from illness faster. And lucky for us, studies have shown that girls are far more likely than guys to keep friendships longer, and have a more diverse circle of friends. Maybe that's why we live longer than guys!

With all the emotional and physical changes we're going through right now, there is no better time to have great friends. Be there for each other—be a shoulder to cry on or an ear to listen. You'll be creating bonds that can last a lifetime!

❀ Girl to Girl

As the saying goes, "The best way to keep a friend is to be a friend." This means always loving and supporting each other, no matter what. However, you can be a good friend while still maintaining your own identity and standards. You don't have to go along with everything your friends are doing, just because they're your friends. If they want to ditch school, for instance, feel free to pass. They'll respect you!

❀ Friendships ....

❀ Did You Know?

It's OK to stop hanging out with a toxic friend, even if she's been a friend for a long time! In a recent survey, almost half (48 percent) of women admitted that "girlfriend clutter"—aka bad friends—has prevented them from spending time with the people they truly care about.

If you have a friend who brings you down or makes bad decisions, stop wasting your time and concentrate on your healthy friendships.

🕐 Helpful Hint

If you want to widen your circle of friends, try volunteering or joining a new class or club. That way you can find girls with your same interests, ambitions, and values.

★ Haley's Question: Silent Treatment!

Help! I made the cheerleading squad and my best friend didn't. Now she will barely talk to me! I told her that my being on the squad won't change our friendship at all, but she just keeps ignoring me and giving me the meanest looks! What can I do?

Emily Says

That's tough, Haley. Your friend probably feels a little jealous that you made the team and she didn't, and also a little afraid that you two will grow apart. She's worried that you will become better friends with your new teammates and leave her in the dust. And really, a lot of friends do grow apart during middle and high school, because people's interests start changing.

Try writing her a letter about why her friendship is so important to you. She'll feel really special.

Isabel Says

The letter is a great idea, but also try giving your friend some space until she cools off. If you keep trying to force her to talk to you, she'll probably just keep shutting you out.

Emily's right Haley, she's not mad at you, she's just hurt that she won't get to share the excitement of being on the squad. When she's ready, she'll come to you.

★ Katie's Question: Crushing

I've been close friends with this guy since we were little kids—he's like my brother. But suddenly, out of nowhere, I think I like him as more than a friend! Now I feel so awkward when we're hanging out! How should I act around him? And how do I find out if he likes me too, without ruining our friendship?

Isabel Says

It's so crazy how you can totally fall for a guy friend in like, the blink of an eye! In my opinion, Katie, you should continue to treat him as a good friend. Talk and laugh with him, just like you always have.

If you want to come clean with your feelings for him, you just have to ask yourself, if he doesn't feel the same way, are you going to be really hurt? Will you be able to go back to being just friends? If you're as close as you say, your friendship should be able to last, no matter how he feels.

Emily Says

This is tricky, Katie! It can be hard to tell if he likes you—mostly because guys are sometimes bad at showing their feelings. If you tell him how you feel, he'll probably be surprised, but really flattered also. And no matter how he feels about you, you should definitely stay friends. You are lucky to have such a good friend of the opposite sex!

> ### ✿ Helpful Hint
>
> It's easy to dash off a quick email or send a text and then feel like you have made the effort to connect with your friends. But, if you want to develop real friendships, you must put time and energy into nurturing them. So meet a friend for a smoothie or go for a walk together. Send him or her a handwritten birthday card in the mail. Going these extra lengths will endear you to the people you care about the most.

> ### ✿ Girl to Girl
>
> It's totally OK to have lots of different groups of friends. You might have friends on your basketball team, in the drama club, and in the "popular group." It is actually really nice to be able to hang out with all kinds of people!

❀ Friendships ....

☞ **Expert's Point of View**

Tips and Advice from Therapist Catherine Butler

Having a healthy, supportive social circle is not only fun but it is beneficial to your well-being.

This is especially true of female friendships. A survey showed that 9 out of 10 women said that being able to talk regularly with their girlfriends is an important part of feeling healthy and balanced in their lives. In addition, 76 percent said they feel happier, 52 percent said they feel reenergized, and 20 percent said they are more successful personally and professionally as a result of being able to talk with their girlfriends regularly.

However, friendships with other females can often be difficult for teenage girls because of jealousy, competitiveness, and gossip. If you can remember the emotional and physical health benefits of having great girlfriends, you will be able to avoid many of these pitfalls!

Wrapping It Up

Every school has cliques. Sometimes, groups of people get together because they share common interests, like they like sports or certain kinds of music. However, some cliques form for really dumb reasons (like how pretty you are) and start excluding other kids just because of how they look or dress. It's closed-minded to be a follower or an elitist—so get to know kids in every group. ★

Girls Rock!

Love, Isabel and Emily

Puberty is a confusing time for all girls, all over the world. No one escapes from the physical and emotional changes that suddenly take over your life. It is unrealistic to think you won't be upset sometimes. Give yourself permission to feel your emotions, including anger, worry, sadness, and fear. Just don't keep them to yourself! Hopefully, reading this book and learning that you are not alone during this tumultuous time has brought you some comfort.

Also, we hope you've figured out that you can't afford to be a bystander in your own life. We were totally happy to help our girlfriends get answers to their difficult questions, but if you have questions that weren't asked in this book, don't be afraid to seek out answers! You can ask your parents, older siblings, friends, teachers, the school nurse, your coach, your doctor, or another adult you think could help you. If you need answers to tough questions, you may also want to meet with a professional counselor, who can give you another level of help and care.

And, if you are still too embarrassed to ask a question in person, the Internet has some chat rooms, message boards, and blogs dedicated to young girls who are going through puberty. Make sure they are legitimate, though, as there is also a lot of bad information on the Internet.

And remember, no Website can ever replace the connection that is forged when you have a face-to-face conversation with a friend or family member that ends with a hug and a smile. So, work to make connections with at least one other person you trust. Developing a puberty "buddy system" can be a lifesaver when you're confused, nervous, or frustrated.

The most important thing *The Ultimate Girl's Guide* has hopefully showed you is that nothing—even puberty—is unmanageable, because you are never alone! Your friends and the people who love you most are here to help. You will get through the frustrating physical changes, the emotional ups and downs, and the tricky social situations and emerge stronger and smarter than ever.

Congratulations on becoming a gorgeous woman!